POCKET
PATRIOT

POCKET
PATRIOT

QUOTES FROM AMERICAN HEROES
EDITED BY KELLY NICKELL

WRITER'S DIGEST BOOKS
Cincinnati, Ohio
www.writersdigest.com

POCKET PATRIOT. © 2005 Writer's Digest Books. Manufactured in the United States of America. All rights reserved. No part of this book may be reproduced in any form or by any electronic or mechanical means including information storage and retrieval systems without permission in writing from the publisher, except by a reviewer, who may quote brief passages in a review. Published by Writer's Digest Books, an imprint of F+W Publications, Inc., 4700 East Galbraith Road, Cincinnati, OH 45236. (800) 289-0963. First edition.

Visit our Web site at www.writersdigest.com for information on more resources for writers.

To receive a free weekly e-mail newsletter delivering tips and updates about writing and about Writer's Digest products, register directly at our Web site at http://newsletters.fwpublications.com.

09 08 07 06 05   5 4 3 2 1

Library of Congress Cataloging-in-Publication Data

Pocket patriot: quotes from American heroes / edited by Kelly Nickell.
　　p. cm.
　Includes index.
　ISBN 1-58297-370-9 (pbk. : alk. paper)
　1. Patriotism—Quotations, maxims, etc. 2. United States—Quotations, maxims, etc.
　I. Nickell, Kelly.
　PN6084.P4P64 2005   2005001263
　323.6'5—dc22

Edited by Kelly Nickell
Designed by Grace Ring
Cover by Clare Finney
Stars Photo by Al Parrish
Man/Flag Photo © 2005 Kamil Vojnar/Photonica
Production Coordinated by Robin Richie

F+W PUBLICATIONS, INC.

TABLE OF CONTENTS

AMERICAN SPIRIT 1

AMERICANS 7

CHALLENGE 11

CHARACTER 16

CITIZENSHIP 30

CIVIL LIBERTIES 37

CIVIL RIGHTS 42

THE CONSTITUTION.............51

COURAGE 53

DEMOCRACY 58

DISSENT 65

DUTY.............................70

EDUCATION 72

ELECTIONS 79

EQUALITY FOR WOMEN 82

FAITH 86

FREEDOM 90

THE FUTURE....................107

GOVERNMENT 114

HOPE 126

IDEALS 132

INGENUITY.....................142

INTERNATIONAL RELATIONS ..145

JUSTICE..........................150

LEADERSHIP 154

PATRIOTISM 160

PEACE............................172

POLITICS 183

POWER 188

THE PRESIDENCY 191

PROGRESS 194

QUALITY OF LIFE 201

SACRIFICE 205

SECURITY 209

SERVICE 214

TERRORISM 219

UNITY 223

WAR.............................232

YOUTH 242

INDEX 245

AMERICAN SPIRIT

Just what is it that America stands for? If she stands for one thing more than another, it is for the sovereignty of self-governing people.

WOODROW WILSON, 28TH PRESIDENT (1913–1921)

The American people make their will known. That will is almost universally a will based on what's right, based on honesty, based on goodness.

COLIN POWELL, FORMER SECRETARY OF STATE

America is never wholly herself unless she is engaged in high moral principle. We as a people have such a purpose today. It is to make kinder the face of the nation and gentler the face of the world.

GEORGE H.W. BUSH, 41ST PRESIDENT (1989–1993)

There is nothing wrong with America that cannot be cured by what is right with America.

WILLIAM J. CLINTON, 42ND PRESIDENT (1993–2001)

Whatever America hopes to bring to pass in the world must first come to pass in the heart of America.

DWIGHT D. EISENHOWER, 34TH PRESIDENT (1953–1961)

Through these acts of compassion, you show that while America's enemies may have injured your bodies, they could not weaken your spirit, or dim your love of country, and your commitment to others.

DICK CHENEY, 46TH VICE PRESIDENT (2001–   )

Americans are not afraid to fight. They fight joyously in a just cause.

HERALD ICKES, FORMER SECRETARY OF THE INTERIOR

We must always remember that America is a great nation today not because of what government did for people but because of what people did for themselves and for one another.

RICHARD M. NIXON, 37TH PRESIDENT (1969–1974)

The genius of the United States is not best or most in its executives or legislatures, nor in its ambassadors or authors or colleges, or churches, or parlors, nor even in its newspapers or inventors, but always most in the common people.

WALT WHITMAN, POET AND ESSAYIST

In America, we say, "Yes, we can."

CONDOLEEZZA RICE, SECRETARY OF STATE AND FORMER NATIONAL SECURITY ADVISOR

We must strive to do what is best—and we must measure our success by what we accomplish not just for one political party or another, not for this or that interest group, but for America and its enduring ideal of liberty and justice for all.

EDWARD M. KENNEDY, U.S. SENATOR

America must be a light to the world, not just a missile.

NANCY PELOSI, MINORITY LEADER OF THE U.S. HOUSE OF REPRESENTATIVES

Therein lies the greatest lesson ever offered to future generations. Never give up, never give in, keep on fighting.

GEORGE H.W. BUSH, 41ST PRESIDENT (1989–1993)

Anyone who will tear down sports will tear down America. Sports and religion have made America what it is today.

WOODY HAYES, FORMER OHIO STATE FOOTBALL COACH

....

America's resilience—the depth of this nation's character—should never be underestimated.

RUDOLPH GIULIANI, FORMER MAYOR OF NEW YORK CITY

....

Americans never quit.

GENERAL DOUGLAS MACARTHUR

If we allow ourselves to believe, without reservation, that we can do what's right and be the better for it—then the best America will become our America.

AL GORE, 45TH VICE PRESIDENT (1993–2001)

We believe that we can best serve our own country and most successfully discharge our obligations to humanity by continuing to be openly and candidly, intensely and scrupulously, American. If we have any heritage, it has been that. If we have any destiny, we have found it in that direction.

CALVIN COOLIDGE, 30TH PRESIDENT (1923–1929)

It is part of the American character to consider nothing as desperate, to surmount every difficulty by resolution and contrivance.

THOMAS JEFFERSON, 3RD PRESIDENT (1801–1809)

No people who have ever lived on this earth have fought harder, paid a higher price for freedom, or done more to advance the dignity of man than the living Americans, those Americans living in this land today.

RONALD REAGAN, 40TH PRESIDENT (1981–1989)

America is not a mere body of traders, it is a body of free men. Our greatness is built upon our freedom—is moral, not material. We have a great ardor for gain; but we have a deep passion for the rights of man.

WOODROW WILSON, 28TH PRESIDENT (1913–1921)

There is nothing wrong with America that the faith, love of freedom, intelligence and energy of her citizens cannot cure.

DWIGHT D. EISENHOWER, 34TH PRESIDENT (1953–1961)

Baseball is an allegorical play about America, a poetic, complex, and subtle play of courage, fear, good luck, mistakes, patience about fate, and sober self-esteem. ... It is impossible to understand America without a thorough knowledge of baseball.

SAUL STEINBERG, ILLUSTRATOR AND CARTOONIST

A truly American sentiment recognizes the dignity of labor and the fact that honor lies in honest toil.

GROVER CLEVELAND, 22ND PRESIDENT (1885–1889) AND 24TH PRESIDENT (1893–1897)

If it will lighten the spirit and add to the resolution with which we take up the task, let me repeat for our Nation, we shall give no people just cause to make war upon us; we hold no national prejudices; we entertain no spirit of revenge; we do not hate; we do not covet; we dream of no conquest, nor boast of armed prowess.

WARREN G. HARDING, 29TH PRESIDENT (1921–1923)

If we are industrious, economical, absolutely fair in our treatment of each other, strictly loyal to our government we, the people, may expect to be prosperous and to remain secure in the enjoyment of all those benefits which this privileged land affords.

GENERAL DOUGLAS MACARTHUR

America is not just a power; it is a promise. It is not enough for our country to be extraordinary in might; it must be exemplary in meaning. Our honor and our role in the world finally depend on the living proof that we are a just society.

NELSON ROCKEFELLER, 41ST VICE PRESIDENT (1974–1977)

I see great things in baseball. It's our game—the American game.

WALT WHITMAN, POET AND ESSAYIST

Americanism means the virtues of courage, honor, justice, truth, sincerity, and hardihood—the virtues that made America.

THEODORE ROOSEVELT, 26TH PRESIDENT (1901–1909)

Our future may lie beyond our vision, but it is not completely beyond our control. It is the shaping impulse of America that neither fate nor nature nor the irresistible tides of history, but the work of our own hands, matched to reason and principle, that will determine our destiny. There is pride in that, even arrogance, but there is also experience and truth. In any event, it is the only way we can live.

ROBERT F. KENNEDY, FORMER ATTORNEY GENERAL AND U.S. SENATOR

When Americans begin a noble cause, we finish it.

CONDOLEEZZA RICE, SECRETARY OF STATE

AMERICANS

Let us ask ourselves, "What kind of people do we think we are?" And let us answer, "Free people, worthy of freedom and determined not only to remain so but to help others gain their freedom as well."

RONALD REAGAN, 40TH PRESIDENT (1981–1989)

I wonder sometimes if we've forgotten who we are. But we're the people who sundered a nation rather than allow a sin called slavery—and we're the people who rose from the ghettoes and the deserts.

GEORGE H.W. BUSH, 41ST PRESIDENT (1989–1993)

Everybody counts. Everybody deserves a chance. Everybody has got a responsibility to fulfill.

WILLIAM J. CLINTON, 42ND PRESIDENT (1993–2001)

The strength of America is her people. You. Me. Us. Our hopes. Our dreams. Our ambitions—and most important, our goodness.

J.C. WATTS, FORMER U.S. REPRESENTATIVE

We Americans are a do-it-yourself people.

RICHARD M. NIXON, 37TH PRESIDENT (1969–1974)

We are the heirs of generations who survived threats much more powerful and awesome than those that challenge us now.

JIMMY CARTER, 39TH PRESIDENT (1977–1981)

Whatever else an American believes or disbelieves about himself, he is absolutely sure he has a sense of humor.

E.B. WHITE, AUTHOR AND ESSAYIST

Sometimes people call me an idealist. Well, that is the way I know I am an American. … America is the only idealist Nation in the world.

WOODROW WILSON, 28TH PRESIDENT (1913–1921)

....

We are one people, all of us pledging allegiance to the stars and stripes, all of us defending the United States of America.

OBAMA BARACK, U.S. SENATOR

....

The American, by nature, is optimistic. He is experimental, an inventor and a builder who builds best when called upon to build greatly.

JOHN F. KENNEDY, 35TH PRESIDENT (1961–1963)

The American Dream is the privilege of being able to realize what you are capable of, at least what you believe you are capable of, and to test yourself, and nobody is going to get in your way.

MIKE WALLACE, BROADCAST JOURNALIST

An American is one who loves justice and believes in the dignity of man. An American is one who will fight for his freedom and that of his neighbor. An American is one who will sacrifice property, ease and security in order that he and his children may retain the rights of free men. An American is one in whose heart is engraved the immortal second sentence of the Declaration of Independence.

HERALD ICKES, FORMER SECRETARY OF THE INTERIOR

Obviously, there's not one American dream. There are hundreds of millions of American dreams.

BOB WOODWARD, INVESTIGATIVE JOURNALIST

The saving grace of America lies in the fact that the overwhelming majority of Americans are possessed of two great qualities—a sense of humor and a sense of proportion.

FRANKLIN DELANO ROOSEVELT, 32ND PRESIDENT (1933–1945)

There is, in every American, I think, something of the old Daniel Boone—who, when he could see the smoke from another chimney, felt himself too crowded and moved further out into the wilderness.

HUBERT HUMPHREY, 38TH VICE PRESIDENT (1965–1969)

Americans will put up with anything provided it doesn't block traffic.

DAN RATHER, BROADCAST JOURNALIST

The confidence that we have always had as a people is not simply some romantic dream. ... It is the idea which founded our Nation and has guided our development as a people.

JIMMY CARTER, 39TH PRESIDENT (1977–1981)

Americans have always assumed, subconsciously, that all problems can be solved, that every story has a happy ending; that the application of enough energy and good will can make everything come out right. In view of our history, this assumption is natural enough. As a people, we have never encountered any obstacle that we could not overcome.

ADLAI STEVENSON, FORMER GOVERNOR OF ILLINOIS AND DIPLOMAT

....

We came from many roots, and we have many branches.

GERALD R. FORD, 38TH PRESIDENT (1974–1977)

....

Individuality, the pride and centripetal isolation of a human being in himself—personalism. ... It forms, or is to form, the compensating balance-wheel of the successful working machinery of aggregate America.

WALT WHITMAN, POET AND ESSAYIST

CHALLENGE

—★—

The challenges of change are always hard. It is important that we begin to unpack those challenges that confront this nation and realize that we each have a role that requires us to change and become more responsible for shaping our own future.

HILLARY RODHAM CLINTON, U.S. SENATOR AND FORMER FIRST LADY

It's lack of faith that makes people afraid of meeting challenges, and I believed in myself.

MUHAMMAD ALI, FORMER WORLD HEAVYWEIGHT CHAMPION

You must accept that you might fail; then, if you do your best and still don't win, at least you can be satisfied that you've tried. If you don't accept failure as a possibility, you don't set high goals, you don't branch out, you don't try—you don't take the risk.

ROSALYN CARTER, FORMER FIRST LADY

Our country faces deep challenges. These challenges we now confront are not Democratic or Republican challenges; they are American challenges that we all must overcome together as one people, as one nation.

AL GORE, 45TH VICE PRESIDENT (1993–2001)

The probability that we may fall in the struggle ought not to deter us from the support of a cause we believe to be just; it shall not deter me.

ABRAHAM LINCOLN, 16TH PRESIDENT (1861–1865)

Perhaps the greatest reward for living a conscious life is that it prepares you to cope with adversity.

CHRISTOPHER REEVE, ACTOR AND DIRECTOR

....

Nothing ever comes to one, that is worth having, except as a result of hard work.

BOOKER T. WASHINGTON, CIVIL RIGHTS REFORMER

....

Freedom, prosperity and peace are not separate principles, or separable policy goals. Each reinforces the other, so serving any one requires an integrated policy that serves all three. The challenges are many, for the world is full of trouble. But it is also full of opportunities, and we are resolved to seize every one of them.

COLIN POWELL, FORMER SECRETARY OF STATE

The world is just what we make it—so let's make ours a great one.

PAT NIXON, FORMER FIRST LADY

We must not be complacent at moments of success, and we must not despair over setbacks. We must learn from our mistakes, improve on our successes, and vanquish this unpardonable enemy.

JOHN MCCAIN, U.S. SENATOR

All of us might wish at times that we lived in a more tranquil world, but we don't. And if our times are difficult and perplexing, so are they challenging and filled with opportunity.

ROBERT F. KENNEDY, FORMER ATTORNEY GENERAL AND U.S. SENATOR

I can accept failure, but I can't accept not trying.

MICHAEL JORDAN, FORMER PROFESSIONAL BASKETBALL PLAYER

Rarely are we met with a challenge, not to our growth or abundance, our welfare or our security, but rather to the values and the purposes and the meaning of our beloved Nation.

LYNDON B. JOHNSON, 36TH PRESIDENT (1963–1969)

The best way to solve any problem is to remove its cause.

MARTIN LUTHER KING, JR., CIVIL RIGHTS LEADER

Far better it is to dare mighty things, to win glorious triumphs, even though checked by failure, than to take rank with those poor spirits who neither enjoy nor suffer much, because they live in the gray twilight that knows not victory or defeat.

THEODORE ROOSEVELT, 26TH PRESIDENT (1901–1909)

Comfort and prosperity have never enriched the world as much as adversity has.

BILLY GRAHAM, CHRISTIAN EVANGELIST

....

Most of the things worth doing in the world had been declared impossible before they were done.

LOUIS BRANDEIS, FORMER U.S. SUPREME COURT ASSOCIATE JUSTICE

The lesson of all this was, of course, that because we're a great nation, our challenges seem complex. It will always be this way. But as long as we remember our first principles and believe in ourselves, the future will always be ours.

RONALD REAGAN, 40TH PRESIDENT (1981–1989)

If you're trying to achieve, there will be roadblocks. I've had them; everybody has had them. But obstacles don't have to stop you. If you run into a wall, don't turn around and give up. Figure out how to climb it, go through it, or work around it.

MICHAEL JORDAN, FORMER PROFESSIONAL BASKETBALL PLAYER

This is our challenge—not to hesitate, not to pause, not to turn about and linger over this evil moment, but to continue on our course so that we may fulfill the destiny that history has set for us.

LYNDON B. JOHNSON, 36TH PRESIDENT (1963–1969)

Where there is no struggle, there is no strength.

Oprah Winfrey, Television Talk-Show Host, Actress, and Producer

Only if you have been in the deepest valley can you ever know how magnificent it is to be on the highest mountain.

Richard M. Nixon, 37th President (1969–1974)

Success in the future will require the same kind of perseverance as well as a healthy dose of courage.

General Henry H. Shelton, Former Chairman of the Joint Chiefs of Staff

You may encounter many defeats, but you must not be defeated. In fact, it may be necessary to encounter the defeats, so you can know who you are, what you can rise from, how you can still come out of it.

Maya Angelou, Poet and Writer

For no quest is worth pursuing that does not require you to pass many tests, take numerous risks.

Robert Ballard, Explorer

Only a man who knows what it is like to be defeated can reach down to the bottom of his soul and come up with the extra ounce of power it takes to win when the match is even.

Muhammad Ali, Former World Heavyweight Champion

CHARACTER

—⋆—

Built into each of us is a little calculator that can make judgments that will never appear on a piece of paper.

COLIN POWELL, FORMER SECRETARY OF STATE

Remember that everyone's life is measured by the power that individual has to make the world better—this is all life is.

BOOKER T. WASHINGTON, EDUCATOR AND CIVIL RIGHTS REFORMER

For most people, life is long enough and varied enough to overcome occasional mistakes and failures.

JOHN McCAIN, U.S. SENATOR

Never lose sight of the fact that the most important yardstick of your success will be how you treat other people—your family, friends, and coworkers, and even strangers you meet along the way.

BARBARA BUSH, FORMER FIRST LADY

The measure of our character is our willingness to give of ourselves for others and for our country.

JOHN KERRY, U.S. SENATOR

Experience should teach us wisdom.

ANDREW JACKSON, 7TH PRESIDENT (1829–1837)

A man does what he must—in spite of personal consequences, in spite of obstacles and dangers and pressures—and that is the basis of all human morality.

JOHN F. KENNEDY, 35TH PRESIDENT (1961–1963)

Don't count the days, make the days count.

MUHAMMAD ALI, FORMER WORLD HEAVYWEIGHT CHAMPION

The greater part of our happiness or misery depends on our dispositions and not our circumstances.

MARTHA WASHINGTON, FORMER FIRST LADY

You can tell a lot about a fellow's character by his way of eating jelly beans.

RONALD REAGAN, 40TH PRESIDENT (1981–1989)

It's important to be able to stand tall, to have the courage of your convictions, and to have resilience if you are up against a disappointment or a temporary defeat.

RALPH NADER, THIRD-PARTY PRESIDENTIAL NOMINEE

Character, in the long run, is the decisive factor in the life of an individual and of nations alike.

THEODORE ROOSEVELT, 26TH PRESIDENT (1901–1909)

....

In matters of principle, stand like a rock; in matters of taste, swim with the current.

THOMAS JEFFERSON, 3RD PRESIDENT (1801–1809)

....

I am not bound to win, but I am bound to be true. I am not bound to succeed, but I am bound to live by the light that I have. I must stand with anybody that stands right, stand with him while he is right, and part with him when he goes wrong.

ABRAHAM LINCOLN, 16TH PRESIDENT (1861–1865)

Integrity is the first step to true greatness.

CHARLES SIMMONS, WRITER AND EDITOR

Character cannot be developed in ease and quiet. Only through experience of trial and suffering can the soul be strengthened, vision cleared, ambition inspired, and success achieved.

HELEN KELLER, SOCIAL ACTIVIST AND AUTHOR

The challenge before you will be to maintain your integrity in a culture that has devalued it.

CHRISTOPHER REEVE, ACTOR AND DIRECTOR

Character is like bells which ring out sweet notes and which, when touched—accidentally even—resound with sweet music.

PHILLIPS BROOKS, EPISCOPAL CLERGYMAN

Character is your moral compass. It sees you safely through the storms of life by providing you with direction.

GENERAL HENRY H. SHELTON, FORMER CHAIRMAN OF THE JOINT CHIEFS OF STAFF

What lies behind us and what lies before us are small matters compared to what lies within us.

RALPH WALDO EMERSON, POET AND ESSAYIST

But rules cannot substitute for character.

ALAN GREENSPAN, U.S. FEDERAL RESERVE BOARD CHAIRMAN

The true measure of an individual is how he treats a person who can do him absolutely no good.

ANN LANDERS, COLUMNIST

Fame is a vapor, popularity an accident, riches take wing. Only one thing endures and that is character.

HORACE GREELEY, NEWSPAPER EDITOR

Every calling is great when greatly pursued.

OLIVER WENDELL HOLMES, JR., FORMER U.S. SUPREME COURT ASSOCIATE JUSTICE

No honesty will make a public man useful if that man is timid or foolish, if he is a hot-headed zealot or an impractical visionary.

THEODORE ROOSEVELT, 26TH PRESIDENT (1901–1909)

Civility is not a sign of weakness, and sincerity is always subject to proof.

JOHN F. KENNEDY, 35TH PRESIDENT (1961–1963)

....

You can go far by being conscientious, but you will go farther and find true satisfaction by being conscious.

CHRISTOPHER REEVE, ACTOR AND DIRECTOR

....

Too many good guys know the truth ... but they lack the guts to join the battle, to be embarrassed, to be criticized, and maybe someday to be beat up in the streets or even martyred.

REAR ADMIRAL JEREMIAH A. DENTON, FORMER U.S. SENATOR

He is rich or poor according to what he is, not according to what he has.

HENRY WARD BEECHER, CONGREGATIONAL CLERGYMAN

There are all too many people, who, in some great period of social change, fail to achieve the new mental outlooks that the new situation demands.

MARTIN LUTHER KING, JR., CIVIL RIGHTS LEADER

Anyone can get to the top by taking shortcuts, by climbing over the bodies of others. But if you take that route, your time at the top will be short-lived.

ROBERT BALLARD, EXPLORER

Now, what should happen when you make a mistake is this: You take your knocks, you learn your lessons, and then you move on.

RONALD REAGAN, 40TH PRESIDENT (1981–1989)

Honesty comes from your natural instinct telling you when you are doing something, whether or not this feels right. You feel a sense of accomplishment and fulfillment and worthiness to the world, in such a way that you know that you are doing the right thing.

OPRAH WINFREY, TELEVISION TALK-SHOW HOST, ACTRESS, AND PRODUCER

You can't build a reputation on what you are going to do.

HENRY FORD, INDUSTRIALIST AND AUTOMOBILE MANUFACTURER

The ultimate is not to win, but to reach within the depths of your capabilities and to compete against yourself to the greatest extent possible. When you do that, you have dignity. You have the pride. You can walk about with character and pride no matter in what place you happen to finish.

BILLY MILLS, OLYMPIC GOLD MEDALIST

Faith in the future, and skepticism about every person or group who offers to lead us there. These conflicting forces work together to shape the American character.

AL GORE, 45TH VICE PRESIDENT (1993–2001)

Cautious, careful people, always casting about to preserve their reputations can never effect a reform.

SUSAN B. ANTHONY, WOMEN'S SUFFRAGE LEADER

No man can always be right. So the struggle is to do one's best; to keep the brain and conscience clear; never to be swayed by unworthy motives or inconsequential reasons, but to strive to unearth the basic factors involved and then do one's duty.

DWIGHT D. EISENHOWER, 34TH PRESIDENT (1953–1961)

Only those who dare to fail greatly, can ever achieve greatly.

ROBERT F. KENNEDY, FORMER ATTORNEY GENERAL AND U.S. SENATOR

The individual can and does make a real difference, even in this increasingly populous, complex world of ours.

SANDRA DAY O'CONNOR, U.S. SUPREME COURT ASSOCIATE JUSTICE

There ain't no free lunches in this country. And don't go spending your whole life commiserating that you got the raw deals. You've got to say, "I think that if I keep working at this and want it bad enough I can have it." It's called perseverance.

LEE IACOCCA, AUTOMOBILE EXECUTIVE

If history teaches anything, it teaches self-delusion in the face of unpleasant facts is folly.

RONALD REAGAN, 40TH PRESIDENT (1981–1989)

Enthusiasm is the yeast that makes your hopes shine to the stars. Enthusiasm is the sparkle in your eyes, the swing in your gait. The grip of your hand, the irresistible surge of will and energy to execute your ideas.

HENRY FORD, INDUSTRIALIST AND AUTOMOBILE MANUFACTURER

Decisions are not irrevocable. Choices do come back.

BARBARA BUSH, FORMER FIRST LADY

We must have the right kind of character—character that makes a man, first of all, a good man in the home, a good father, a good husband—that makes a man a good neighbor.

THEODORE ROOSEVELT, 26TH PRESIDENT (1901–1909)

Perseverance is the hard work you do after you get tired of doing the hard work you already did.

NEWT GINGRICH, FORMER SPEAKER OF THE HOUSE OF REPRESENTATIVES

You know, by the time you reach my age, you've made plenty of mistakes. And if you've lived your life properly, you learn. You put things in perspective. You pull your energies together. You change. You go forward.

RONALD REAGAN, 40TH PRESIDENT (1981–1989)

When wealth is lost, nothing is lost; when health is lost, something is lost; when character is lost, all is lost.

BILLY GRAHAM, CHRISTIAN EVANGELIST

As simple as it sounds, we all must try to be the best person we can: by making the best choices, by making the most of the talents we've been given.

MARY LOU RETTON, OLYMPIC GOLD MEDALIST

Always do more than is required of you.

GENERAL GEORGE S. PATTON

I am rather inclined to silence, and whether that be wise or not, it is at least more unusual nowadays to find a man who can hold his tongue than to find one who cannot.

ABRAHAM LINCOLN, 16TH PRESIDENT (1861–1865)

An epidemic of indiscriminate assault upon character does not good, but very great harm.

THEODORE ROOSEVELT, 26TH PRESIDENT (1901–1909)

....

All tyranny needs to gain a foothold is for people of good conscience to remain silent.

THOMAS JEFFERSON, 3RD PRESIDENT (1801–1809)

....

Follow your instincts. That's where true wisdom manifests itself.

OPRAH WINFREY, TELEVISION TALK-SHOW HOST, ACTRESS, AND PRODUCER

Every day we have to make decisions. It is through this decision making process that we show those around us the quality of our character.

GENERAL CHARLES C. KRULAK

As I grow older, I pay less attention to what men say. I just watch what they do.

ANDREW CARNEGIE, INDUSTRIALIST AND PHILANTHROPIST

If the power to do hard work is not a skill, it's the best possible substitute for it.

JAMES GARFIELD, 20TH PRESIDENT (1881)

Morale is the state of mind. It is steadfastness and courage and hope. It is confidence and zeal and loyalty. It is élan, esprit de corps and determination.

GENERAL GEORGE C. MARSHALL, FORMER SECRETARY OF DEFENSE

That's all a man can hope for during his lifetime—to set an example—and when he is dead, to be an inspiration for history.

WILLIAM MCKINLEY, 25TH PRESIDENT (1897–1901)

Life is a series of experiences, each one of which makes us bigger, even though sometimes it is hard to realize this. For the world was built to develop character, and we must learn that the setbacks and griefs which we endure help us in our marching onward.

HENRY FORD, INDUSTRIALIST AND AUTOMOBILE MANUFACTURER

If you'll not settle for anything less than your best, you will be amazed at what you can accomplish in your lives.

VINCE LOMBARDI, FORMER FOOTBALL COACH

There are no secrets to success—don't waste time looking for them. Success is the result of perfection, hard work, learning from failure, loyalty to those for whom you work, and persistence.

COLIN POWELL, FORMER SECRETARY OF STATE

Always bear in mind that your own resolution to succeed is more important than any other.

ABRAHAM LINCOLN, 16TH PRESIDENT (1861–1865)

Today as the fabric of society is saturated with complaint and protest, each of you has the opportunity to be a hero. Do what you know must be done.
CLARENCE THOMAS, U.S. SUPREME COURT ASSOCIATE JUSTICE

Always make a total effort, even when the odds are against you.
ARNOLD PALMER, PROFESSIONAL GOLFER

Always give your best. Never get discouraged. Never be petty. Always remember, others may hate you. Those who hate you don't win unless you hate them. And then you destroy yourself.
RICHARD M. NIXON, 37TH PRESIDENT (1969–1974)

We cannot afford to accumulate a deficit in the books of human fortitude.
FRANKLIN DELANO ROOSEVELT, 32ND PRESIDENT (1933–1945)

Life is not a spectator sport. … If you're going to spend your whole life in the grandstand just watching what goes on, in my opinion you're wasting your life.
JACKIE ROBINSON, FORMER PROFESSIONAL BASEBALL PLAYER

Be more concerned with your character than your reputation, because your character is what you really are, while your reputation is merely what others think you are.

JOHN WOODEN, FORMER COLLEGE BASKETBALL COACH

If you are going to achieve excellence in big things, you develop the habit in little matters. Excellence is not an exception, it is a prevailing attitude.

COLIN POWELL, FORMER SECRETARY OF STATE

If you think you can do a thing or think you can't do a thing, you're right.

HENRY FORD, INDUSTRIALIST AND AUTOMOBILE MANUFACTURER

Do you want to know who you are? Don't ask. Act! Action will delineate and define you.

THOMAS JEFFERSON, 3RD PRESIDENT (1801–1809)

....

No man is defeated without until he has first been defeated within.

ELEANOR ROOSEVELT, FORMER FIRST LADY

....

He that cannot reason is a fool. He that will not is a bigot. He that dare not is a slave.

ANDREW CARNEGIE, INDUSTRIALIST AND PHILANTHROPIST

Adversity is sometimes hard upon a man; but for one man who can stand prosperity, there are a hundred that will stand adversity.

ELVIS PRESLEY, SINGER AND ACTOR

The greatest accomplishment is not in never falling, but in rising again after you fall.

VINCE LOMBARDI, FORMER FOOTBALL COACH

I do not think that there is any other quality so essential to success of any kind as the quality of perseverance. It overcomes almost everything, even nature.

JOHN D. ROCKEFELLER, INDUSTRIALIST

Press on: Nothing in the world can take the place of perseverance. Talent will not; nothing is more common than unsuccessful men with talent. Genius will not; unrewarded genius is almost a proverb. Education will not; the world is full of educated derelicts. Persistence and determination alone are omnipotent.

CALVIN COOLIDGE, 30TH PRESIDENT (1923–1929)

You never really understand a person until you consider things from his point of view.

HARPER LEE, PULITZER PRIZE-WINNING AUTHOR

Apathy has no adventures. Cynicism leaves no monuments.

GEORGE W. BUSH, 43RD PRESIDENT (2001–   )

CITIZENSHIP

—★—

Nothing strengthens the judgment and quickens the conscience like individual responsibility.

ELIZABETH CADY STANTON, WOMEN'S SUFFRAGE LEADER

Let your voice be heard.

JIMMY CARTER, 39TH PRESIDENT (1977–1981)

There can be no daily democracy without daily citizenship.

RALPH NADER, THIRD-PARTY PRESIDENTIAL NOMINEE

Liberty does not consist … in mere declarations of the rights of man. It consists in the translation of those declarations in to definite actions.

WOODROW WILSON, 28TH PRESIDENT (1913–1921)

Every citizen owes to the country a vigilant watch and close scrutiny of its public servants and a fair and reasonable estimate of their fidelity and usefulness. Thus is the people's will impressed upon the whole framework of our civil polity—municipal, State, and Federal; and this is the price of our liberty and the inspiration of our faith in the Republic.

GROVER CLEVELAND, 22ND PRESIDENT (1885–1889) AND 24TH PRESIDENT (1893–1897)

As men and women of character and of faith in the soundness of democratic methods, we must work like dogs to justify that faith.

DWIGHT D. EISENHOWER, 34TH PRESIDENT (1953–1961)

Since the days of Greece and Rome when the word "citizen" was a title of honor, we have often seen more emphasis put on the rights of citizenship than on its responsibilities. And today, as never before in the free world, responsibility is the greatest right of citizenship and service is the greatest of freedom's privileges.

ROBERT F. KENNEDY, FORMER ATTORNEY GENERAL AND U.S. SENATOR

....

Citizenship is the prime test in the welfare of the nation.

THEODORE ROOSEVELT, 26TH PRESIDENT (1901–1909)

....

Words without actions are the assassins of idealism.

HERBERT HOOVER, 31ST PRESIDENT (1929–1933)

For those of us who as citizens of this nation have been blessed with treasure, and wealth, and good position, and comfortable homes, and all the blessings of this land, to be a good citizen, to be a big citizen, requires you to do more in the way of sharing with those who are in need.

COLIN POWELL, FORMER SECRETARY OF STATE

The humblest citizen in all the land, when clad in the armor of a righteous cause, is stronger than all the hosts of error.

WILLIAM JENNINGS BRYAN, STATESMAN

Women should get into politics. They should take more active part in civic affairs, give up some of their time ... for their duty as citizens. Whether we are wanted in politics or not, we are here to stay and [the] only force that can put us out is that which gave us the vote. The vote itself is not a perfect utility. It is only perfected in the way in which it is used.

LOU HENRY HOOVER, FORMER FIRST LADY

Citizenship requires skills like any other occupation or profession, and it's good to learn on the job.

RALPH NADER, THIRD-PARTY PRESIDENTIAL NOMINEE

You will be judged by what kind of citizen you are.

DONNA E. SHALALA, FORMER SEC. OF HEALTH AND HUMAN SERVICES

Every good citizen makes his country's honor his own and cherishes it not only as precious but as sacred. He is willing to risk his life in its defense and is conscious that he gains protection while he gives it.

ANDREW JACKSON, 7TH PRESIDENT (1829–1837)

America needs more than taxpayers, spectators, and occasional voters. America needs full-time citizens.

GEORGE W. BUSH, 43RD PRESIDENT (2001–   )

....

Whatever affects one directly, affects all indirectly.

MARTIN LUTHER KING, JR., CIVIL RIGHTS LEADER

....

As citizens come together to plan their common future—as they realize that they can make a difference right in their own neighborhoods—we open the door to more vibrant civic life and self–government on a much broader scale.

AL GORE, 45TH VICE PRESIDENT (1993–2001)

America will never be destroyed from the outside. If we falter and lose our freedoms, it will be because we destroyed ourselves.

ABRAHAM LINCOLN, 16TH PRESIDENT (1861–1865)

Never doubt that a small group of thoughtful, committed citizens can change the world; indeed, it's the only thing that ever has.

MARGARET MEAD, ANTHROPOLOGIST

It is time for all of us to live up more fully to the concept of citizenship.

COLIN POWELL, FORMER SECRETARY OF STATE

The only title in our democracy superior to that of President is the title of citizen.

LOUIS BRANDEIS, FORMER U.S. SUPREME COURT ASSOCIATE JUSTICE

....

Our citizenship in the United States is our national character. Our citizenship in any particular state is only our local distinction. By the latter we are known at home, by the former to the world. Our great title is *Americans*—our inferior one varies with the place.

THOMAS PAINE, AMERICAN REVOLUTIONARY

Consider the rights of others before your own feelings, and the feelings of others before your own rights.

JOHN WOODEN, FORMER COLLEGE BASKETBALL COACH

Knowledge about the ideas embodied in the Constitution and the ways in which it shapes our lives is not passed down from generation to generation through the gene pool; it must be learned anew by each generation. It is not enough simply to read or memorize the Constitution. Rather, we should try to understand the ideas that gave it life and that give it strength still today.

SANDRA DAY O'CONNOR, U.S. SUPREME COURT ASSOCIATE JUSTICE

No man can be a good citizen unless he has a wage more than sufficient to cover the bare cost of living.

THEODORE ROOSEVELT, 26TH PRESIDENT (1901–1909)

How imperious, then, is the obligation imposed upon every citizen, in his own sphere of action, whether limited or extended, to exert himself in perpetuating a condition of things so singularly happy! All the lessons of history and experience must be lost upon us if we are content to trust alone to the peculiar advantages we happen to possess.

MARTIN VAN BUREN, 8TH PRESIDENT (1837–1841)

Get involved in some of the big ideas of your time.

BARBARA BUSH, FORMER FIRST LADY

Perhaps it is impossible for a person who does no good to do no harm.

HARRIET BEECHER STOWE, AUTHOR

The beauty of citizen involvement is that when your horizon expands, and you think more of your own personal significance, then all your little personal hang-ups, which loomed so large in your daily life, suddenly begin to recede and fall and melt away.

RALPH NADER, THIRD-PARTY PRESIDENTIAL NOMINEE

The first requisite of a good citizen in this republic of ours is that he should be able and willing to pull his weight.

THEODORE ROOSEVELT, 26TH PRESIDENT (1901–1909)

Life always rides in strength to victory, not through internationalism ... but only through the direct responsibility of the individual.

FRANK LLOYD WRIGHT, ARCHITECT

....

What you don't do can be a destructive force.

ELEANOR ROOSEVELT, FORMER FIRST LADY

....

CIVIL LIBERTIES

———★———

The liberty of the press is essential to the security of freedom in a state.

JOHN ADAMS, 1ST VICE PRESIDENT (1789–1797) AND 2ND PRESIDENT (1797–1801)

America is committed to seeing civil liberties protected as a shield for freedom-loving people, not as a sword for freedom-loathing people.

JOHN ASHCROFT, FORMER U.S. ATTORNEY GENERAL

Newspapers are the schoolmasters of the common people. That endless book, the newspaper, is our national glory.

HENRY WARD BEECHER, CONGREGATIONAL CLERGYMAN

I believe in the dignity of labor, whether with head or hand; that the world owes no man a living but that it owes every man an opportunity to make a living.

JOHN D. ROCKEFELLER, INDUSTRIALIST

Individuality is the aim of political liberty. By leaving to the citizen as much freedom of action and of being as comports with order and the rights of others, the institutions render him truly a free man. He is left to pursue his means of happiness in his own manner.

JAMES FENNIMORE COOPER, NOVELIST

I'm neutral in this race but I'm for freedom of speech, which means people should be able to assemble and speak without being shouted down.

AL FRANKEN, AUTHOR AND COMMENTATOR

"Civil Liberties" emphasizes the liberty of the individual.

ELEANOR ROOSEVELT, FORMER FIRST LADY

More than in times of peace it is necessary that the channels for free public discussion of governmental policies shall be open and unclogged.

ROBERT "FIGHTIN' BOB" LAFOLLETTE, FORMER U.S. SENATOR

Where the press is free, and every man able to read, all is safe.

THOMAS JEFFERSON, 3RD PRESIDENT (1801–1809)

The first principle of a free society is an untrammeled flow of words in an open forum.

ADLAI STEVENSON, FORMER GOVERNOR OF ILLINOIS AND DIPLOMAT

All are free to believe or not believe; all are free to practice a faith or not. But those who believe must be free to speak of and act on their belief, to apply moral teaching to public questions.

RONALD REAGAN, 40TH PRESIDENT (1981–1989)

A popular Government, without popular information, or the means of acquiring it, is but a prologue to a farce or a tragedy; or perhaps both.

JAMES MADISON, 4TH PRESIDENT (1809–1817)

There must be no barriers for freedom of inquiry. There is no place for dogma in science. The scientist is free, and must be free to ask any question, to doubt any assertion, to seek for any evidence, to correct any errors.

J. ROBERT OPPENHEIMER, PHYSICIST

Laws alone cannot secure freedom of expression; in order that every man present his views without penalty there must be a spirit of tolerance in the entire population.

ALBERT EINSTEIN, NOBEL PRIZE-WINNING PHYSICIST

If the freedom of speech is taken away then dumb and silent we may be led, like sheep to the slaughter.

GEORGE WASHINGTON, 1ST PRESIDENT (1789–1797)

Every right implies a responsibility, every opportunity, an obligation, every possession, a duty.

JOHN D. ROCKEFELLER, INDUSTRIALIST

Our liberty depends on the freedom of the press, and that cannot be limited without being lost.

THOMAS JEFFERSON, 3RD PRESIDENT (1801–1809)

....

The sources of information are the springs from which democracy drinks.

ADLAI STEVENSON, FORMER GOVERNOR OF ILLINOIS AND DIPLOMAT

Next to the right of liberty, the right of property is the most important individual right guaranteed by the Constitution and the one which, united with that of personal liberty, has contributed more to the growth of civilization than any other institution established by the human race.

WILLIAM HOWARD TAFT, 27TH PRESIDENT (1909–1913)

Free speech does not live many hours after free industry and free commerce die.

HERBERT HOOVER, 31ST PRESIDENT (1929–1933)

We basically do have a free press that we can operate independently. But the real input comes from people who believe in a free press, believe in the First Amendment, believe in open discourse as much as possible, hate secrets, hate secret government, hate secret concentrations of power.

BOB WOODWARD, INVESTIGATIVE JOURNALIST

Literature becomes free institutions. It is the graceful ornament of civil liberty, and a happy restraint on the asperities which political controversies sometimes occasion.

DANIEL WEBSTER, STATESMAN AND LAWYER

If the 1st Amendment means anything, it means that a state has no business telling a man, sitting alone in his own house, what books he may read or what films he may watch.

THURGOOD MARSHALL, FORMER U.S. SUPREME COURT ASSOCIATE JUSTICE

Librarians see themselves as guardians of the First Amendment. You got a thousand Mother Joneses at the barricades! I love the librarians and I am grateful for them!

MICHAEL MOORE, DOCUMENTARY FILMMAKER AND AUTHOR

....

As long as men are free to ask what they must, free to say what they think, free to think what they will, freedom can never be lost.

J. ROBERT OPPENHEIMER, PHYSICIST

CIVIL RIGHTS

America is not like a blanket—one piece of unbroken cloth, the same color, the same texture, the same size. America is more like a quilt: many patches, many pieces, many colors, many sizes, all woven and held together by a common thread.

JESSE JACKSON, CIVIL RIGHTS LEADER

The nation is sick, trouble is in the land, confusion all around. That's a strange statement. But I know, somehow, that only when it is dark enough can you see the stars.

MARTIN LUTHER KING, JR., CIVIL RIGHTS LEADER

There is in this country no superior, dominant, ruling class of citizens. There is no caste here. Our Constitution is color-blind, and neither knows nor tolerates classes among citizens. In respect of civil rights, all citizens are equal before the law.

JOHN MARSHALL HARLAN, FORMER U.S. SUPREME COURT ASSOCIATE JUSTICE

There are those who say to you—we are rushing this issue of civil rights. I say we are 172 years late.

HUBERT HUMPHREY, 38TH VICE PRESIDENT (1965–1969)

We claim for ourselves every single right that belongs to a freeborn American, political, civil and social; and until we get these rights we will never cease to protest and assail the ears of America!

W.E.B. DuBois, Sociologist and Civil Rights Leader

I had reasoned this out in my mind, there was two things I had a right to, liberty and death. If I could not have one, I would have the other, for no man should take me alive.

Harriet Tubman, Abolitionist

There is no room in baseball for discrimination. It is our national pastime and a game for all.

Lou Gherig, Former Professional Baseball Player

....

The only tired I was, was tired of giving in.

Rosa Parks, Civil Rights Pioneer, on refusing to give up her seat on the bus to a white male

....

We will not accept the peace of stifled rights, or the order imposed by fear, or the unity that stifles protest. For peace cannot be purchased at the cost of liberty.

Lyndon B. Johnson, 36th President (1963–1969)

On this generation of Americans falls the burden of proving to the world that we really mean it when we say all men are created free and are equal before the law.

ROBERT F. KENNEDY, FORMER ATTORNEY GENERAL

....

I am America. I am the part you won't recognize. But get used to me. Black, confident, cocky; my name, not yours; my religion, not yours; my goals, my own; get used to me.

MUHAMMAD ALI, FORMER WORLD HEAVYWEIGHT CHAMPION

Let me implore you to teach the members of our race everywhere that they must become, in an increasing degree, creators of their own careers.

BOOKER T. WASHINGTON, EDUCATOR AND CIVIL RIGHTS REFORMER

Let us stand with a greater determination. And let us move on in these powerful days, these days of challenge, to make America what it ought to be. We have an opportunity to make America a better nation.

MARTIN LUTHER KING, JR., CIVIL RIGHTS LEADER

There is no cause for self-satisfaction in the long denial of equal rights of millions of Americans. But there is cause for hope and for faith in our democracy.

LYNDON B. JOHNSON, 36TH PRESIDENT (1963–1969)

Wherever there is a human being, I see God-given rights inherent in that being, whatever may be the sex or complexion.

WILLIAM LLOYD GARRISON, ABOLITIONIST

This is a world of compensations; and he who would be no slave, must consent to have no slave. Those who deny freedom to others deserve it not for themselves. ...

ABRAHAM LINCOLN, 16TH PRESIDENT (1861–1865)

To be black and conscious in America is to be in a constant state of rage.

JAMES BALDWIN, ESSAYIST, NOVELIST, AND PLAYWRIGHT

....

The destiny of colored America ... is the destiny of America.

FREDERICK DOUGLASS, ABOLITIONIST AND AUTOBIOGRAPHER

....

The civil rights struggle was America's chance to resolve the contradictions inherent in its birth.

CONDOLEEZZA RICE, SECRETARY OF STATE AND FORMER NATIONAL SECURITY ADVISOR

Slavery always has, and always will, produce insurrections wherever it exists, because it is a violation of the natural order of things.

ANGELINA GRIMKÉ, ABOLITIONIST AND WOMEN'S RIGHTS ADVOCATE

We must recognize the full human equality of all our people—before God, before the law, and in the councils of government. ... We must do it for the single and fundamental reason that it is the right thing to do.

ROBERT F. KENNEDY, FORMER ATTORNEY GENERAL AND U.S. SENATOR

For at the real heart for equality is a deep-seated belief in the democratic process.

LYNDON B. JOHNSON, 36TH PRESIDENT (1963–1969)

....

Our victories in the past have come to us through our ability to be calm and patient, often while enduring great wrong.

BOOKER T. WASHINGTON, CIVIL RIGHTS REFORMER

....

If we cannot end now our differences, at least we can help make the world safe for diversity.

JOHN F. KENNEDY, 35TH PRESIDENT (1961–1963)

Who ever walked behind anyone to freedom? If we can't go hand in hand, I don't want to go.

HAZEL SCOTT, JAZZ PIANIST AND SINGER

....

There is nothing more dangerous than to build a society, with a large segment of people in that society, who feel that they have no stake in it; who feel that they have nothing to lose. People who have a stake in their society, protect that society, but when they don't have it, they unconsciously want to destroy it.

MARTIN LUTHER KING, JR., CIVIL RIGHTS LEADER

I want to let you know that all of us should be free and have equal opportunity and that is what I'm trying to instill and encourage and inspire young people to reach their highest potential.

ROSA PARKS, CIVIL RIGHTS PIONEER

How can we love our country and not love our countrymen; and loving them, reach out a hand when they fall, heal them when they're sick, and provide opportunity to make them self-sufficient so they will be equal in fact and not just in theory?

RONALD REAGAN, 40TH PRESIDENT (1981–1989)

Racism is a human problem and a crime that is absolutely so ghastly that a person who is fighting racism is well within his rights to fight against it by any means necessary until it is eliminated.

MALCOLM X, MUSLIM LEADER

[This] is the land of the free and the home of the brave, and I believe it should be just that for all people. They can think of themselves as human beings and they'll enjoy the blessings of the freedom of this country.

ROSA PARKS, CIVIL RIGHTS PIONEER

No race can prosper till it learns that there is as much dignity in tilling a field as in writing a poem. It is at the bottom of life we must begin, and not at the top. Nor should we permit our grievances to overshadow our opportunities.

BOOKER T. WASHINGTON, EDUCATOR AND CIVIL RIGHTS REFORMER

In order for America to be 100 percent strong—economically, defensively, and morally—we cannot afford the waste of having second- and third-class citizens.

JACKIE ROBINSON, FORMER PROFESSIONAL BASEBALL PLAYER

To deny a man his hopes because of his color or race, his religion or the place of his birth is not only to do injustice, it is to deny America and to dishonor the dead who gave their lives for American freedom.

LYNDON B. JOHNSON, 36TH PRESIDENT (1963–1969)

··

Whenever I hear anyone arguing for slavery, I feel a strong impulse to see it tried on him personally.

ABRAHAM LINCOLN, 16TH PRESIDENT (1861–1865)

··

I have come here today not in anger or to anger, though my mere presence has been sufficient, obviously, to anger some. Nor have I come to defend my views, but rather to assert my right to think for myself, to refuse to have my ideas assigned to me as though I was an intellectual slave because I'm black. I come to state that I'm a man, free to think for myself and do as I please.

CLARENCE THOMAS, U.S. SUPREME COURT ASSOCIATE JUSTICE

We are men; we will be treated as men. On this rock we have planted our banners. We will never give up, though the trump of doom finds us still fighting.

W.E.B. DUBOIS, SOCIOLOGIST AND CIVIL RIGHTS LEADER

There is no defense or security for any of us except in the highest intelligence and development of all.

BOOKER T. WASHINGTON, EDUCATOR AND CIVIL RIGHTS REFORMER

Nobody can give you freedom. Nobody can give you equality or justice or anything. If you're a man, you take it.

MALCOLM X, MUSLIM LEADER

....

I realize that I'm black, but I like to be viewed as a person, and this is everybody's wish.

MICHAEL JORDAN, FORMER PROFESSIONAL BASKETBALL PLAYER

....

The cost of liberty is less than the price of repression.

W.E.B. DuBois, SOCIOLOGIST AND CIVIL RIGHTS LEADER

THE CONSTITUTION

The Constitution of the United States was made not merely for the generation that then existed, but for posterity—unlimited, undefined, endless, perpetual posterity.

HENRY CLAY, U.S. STATESMAN

To live under the American Constitution is the greatest political privilege that was ever accorded to the human race.

CALVIN COOLIDGE, 30TH PRESIDENT (1923–1929)

Our Constitution is so simple and practical that it is possible always to meet extraordinary needs by changes in emphasis and arrangement without loss of essential form.

FRANKLIN DELANO ROOSEVELT, 32ND PRESIDENT (1933–1945)

The court is really the keeper of the conscience, and the conscience is the Constitution.

DWIGHT D. EISENHOWER, 34TH PRESIDENT (1953–1961)

The Constitution … is unquestionably the wisest ever yet presented to men.

THOMAS JEFFERSON, 3RD PRESIDENT (1801–1809)

Our constitution works. Our great republic is a government of laws, not of men.

GERALD R. FORD, 38TH PRESIDENT (1974–1977)

The United States Constitution has proved itself the most marvelously elastic compilation of rules of government ever written.

FRANKLIN DELANO ROOSEVELT, 32ND PRESIDENT (1933–1945)

The Constitution is not an instrument for the government to restrain the people, it is an instrument for the people to restrain the government—lest it come to dominate our lives and interests.

PATRICK HENRY, AMERICAN REVOLUTIONARY LEADER

....

The Constitution only gives people the right to pursue happiness. You have to catch it yourself.

BENJAMIN FRANKLIN, STATESMAN AND SCIENTIST

....

Constitutions should consist only of general provisions; the reason is that they must necessarily be permanent, and that they cannot calculate for the possible change of things.

ALEXANDER HAMILTON, U.S. STATESMAN

COURAGE

True courage is being afraid, and going ahead and doing your job anyhow, that's what courage is.

GENERAL H. NORMAN SCHWARZKOPF

I have learned over the years that when one's mind is made up, this diminishes fear; knowing what must be done does away with fear.

ROSA PARKS, CIVIL RIGHTS PIONEER

Real courage is when you know you're licked before you begin, but you begin anyway and see it through no matter what.

HARPER LEE, PULITZER PRIZE-WINNING AUTHOR

One man with courage makes a majority.

ANDREW JACKSON, 7TH PRESIDENT (1829–1837)

In our blessed and progressive society there may be fewer occasions when we need to be afraid to be virtuous, when we need our courage to remain so, but still they are more numerous than the occasions when we need something more than our conscience, when we need physical strength and skill to act.

JOHN MCCAIN, U.S. SENATOR

Those who test our courage will find it strong, and those who seek our friendship will find it honorable.

LYNDON B. JOHNSON, 36TH PRESIDENT (1963–1969)

··

It doesn't take a hero to order men into battle. It takes a hero to be one of those men who goes into battle.

GENERAL H. NORMAN SCHWARZKOPF

··

Those who have the courage to face up to ethical challenges in their daily lives will find that same courage can be drawn upon in times of great stress, in times of great controversy, in the never ending battle between good and evil.

GENERAL CHARLES C. KRULAK

He who is not courageous enough to take risks will accomplish nothing in life.

MUHAMMAD ALI, FORMER WORLD HEAVYWEIGHT CHAMPION

Courage, considered in itself or without reference to its causes, is no virtue, and deserves no esteem. It is found in the best and the worst, and is to be judged according to the qualities from which it springs and with which it is conjoined.

WILLIAM ELLERY CHANNING, UNITARIAN CLERGYMAN

Heroism feels and never reasons and therefore is always right.

RALPH WALDO EMERSON, POET AND ESSAYIST

No arsenal or no weapon in the arsenals of the world is so formidable as the will and moral courage of free men and women.

RONALD REAGAN, 40TH PRESIDENT (1981–1989)

If you don't have the courage to keep your virtue when facing unwanted consequences, you're not virtuous.

JOHN McCAIN, U.S. SENATOR

You gain strength, courage, and confidence by every experience in which you really stop to look fear in the face. You must do the thing which you think you cannot do.

ELEANOR ROOSEVELT, FORMER FIRST LADY AND UNITED NATIONS DELEGATE

....

Courage is the price that life exacts for granting peace.

AMELIA EARHART, AVIATION PIONEER

....

Courage is contagious. When a brave man takes a stand, the spines of others are often stiffened.

BILLY GRAHAM, CHRISTIAN EVANGELIST

The only thing we have to fear is fear itself—nameless, unreasoning, unjustified terror which paralyzes needed efforts to convert retreat into advance.

FRANKLIN DELANO ROOSEVELT, 32ND PRESIDENT (1933–1945)

Courage is being afraid but going on anyhow.

DAN RATHER, BROADCAST JOURNALIST

Listen to the truths that lie within your hearts, and be not afraid to follow them wherever they may lead you. Those three little words hold the power to transform individuals and change the world. They can supply the quiet resolve and unvoiced courage necessary to endure the inevitable intimidation.

CLARENCE THOMAS, U.S. SUPREME COURT ASSOCIATE JUSTICE

One isn't necessarily born with courage, but one is born with potential. Without courage, we cannot practice any other virtue with consistency. We can't be kind, true, merciful, generous, or honest.

MAYA ANGELOU, POET AND WRITER

....

The only thing necessary for the triumph of evil is for good men—and good women—to do nothing.

LADY BIRD JOHNSON, FORMER FIRST LADY

I would define true courage to be a perfect sensibility of the measure of danger, and a mental willingness to endure it.

WILLIAM TECUMSEH SHERMAN, CIVIL WAR GENERAL

America cannot be an ostrich with its head in the sand.

WOODROW WILSON, 28TH PRESIDENT (1913–1921)

You must have the courage to stand for those convictions that will earn you contempt today from all the powers that be.

ALAN KEYES, FORMER U.S. REPRESENTATIVE TO THE UNITED NATIONS

There are no easy answers ... but there are simple answers. We must have the courage to do what we know is morally right.

RONALD REAGAN, 40TH PRESIDENT (1981–1989)

DEMOCRACY

———★———

Every American owns all America.
OLIVER WENDELL HOLMES, PHYSICIAN, POET, AND HUMORIST

While democracy in the long run is the most stable form of government, in the short run, it is among the most fragile.
MADELEINE ALBRIGHT, FORMER SECRETARY OF STATE

In our democracy, the future is not something that just happens to us; it is something we make for ourselves—together.
AL GORE, 45TH VICE PRESIDENT (1993–2001)

Here in a democracy, the government still exists for the individual, but that does not mean that we do not have to watch and that we do not have to examine ourselves to be sure that we preserve the civil liberties for all our people, which are the basis of our democracy.
ELEANOR ROOSEVELT, FORMER FIRST LADY AND UNITED NATIONS DELEGATE

I shall on all subjects have a policy to recommend, but none to enforce against the will of the people.
ULYSSES S. GRANT, 18TH PRESIDENT (1869–1877)

We do not distrust the future of essential democracy.

FRANKLIN DELANO ROOSEVELT, 32ND PRESIDENT (1933–1945)

The world must be made safe for democracy. Its peace must be planted upon the tested foundations of political liberty.

WOODROW WILSON, 28TH PRESIDENT (1913–1921)

We want democracy to survive for all generations to come, not to become the insolvent phantom of tomorrow.

DWIGHT D. EISENHOWER, 34TH PRESIDENT (1953–1961)

....

The vitality of our democracy depends on the active participation of each generation of citizens.

JOHN GLENN, FORMER SENATOR AND ASTRONAUT

....

I profoundly believe that the future of our world is not to be found in authoritarianism that wears the mask of order, or totalitarianism that wears the mask of justice. Instead, let us find our future in the human face of democracy, the human voice of individual liberty, the human hand of economic development.

JIMMY CARTER, 39TH PRESIDENT (1977–1981)

It is not enough to merely defend democracy. To defend it may be to lose it; to extend it is to strengthen it. Democracy is not property; it is an idea.

HUBERT HUMPHREY, 38TH VICE PRESIDENT (1965–1969)

As I would not be a slave, so I would not be a master. This expresses my idea of democracy.

ABRAHAM LINCOLN, 16TH PRESIDENT (1861–1865)

Democracy alone can supply the vitalizing force to stir the peoples of the world into triumphant action, not only against their human oppressors, but also against their ancient enemies—hunger, misery, and despair.

HARRY S. TRUMAN, 33RD PRESIDENT (1945–1953)

Morality is truly the only alternative to barbarism, and is required not only for nations, especially those with democratic forms of government to exist, but for civilization itself to exist.

REAR ADMIRAL JEREMIAH A. DENTON, FORMER U.S. SENATOR

Democracy stands or falls on a mutual trust—government's trust of the people and the people's trust of the governments they elect.

AL GORE, 45TH VICE PRESIDENT (1993–2001)

We always believed that we were part of a great movement of humanity itself called democracy, involved in the search for freedom, and that belief has always strengthened us in our progress.

JIMMY CARTER, 39TH PRESIDENT (1977–1981)

Yet we can maintain a free society only if we recognize that in a free society no one can win all the time. No one can have his own way all the time, and no one is right all the time.

RICHARD M. NIXON, 37TH PRESIDENT (1969–1974)

Optimism comes less easily today, not because democracy is less vigorous, but because democracy's enemies have refined their instruments of repression.

RONALD REAGAN, 40TH PRESIDENT (1981–1989)

....

Our democracy is still a work in progress, not a finished product. The hard work begins anew each day.

CONDOLEEZZA RICE, SECRETARY OF STATE

....

There is nothing mysterious about the foundations of a healthy and strong democracy.

FRANKLIN DELANO ROOSEVELT, 32ND PRESIDENT (1933–1945)

Democracy is no easy form of government. Few nations have been able to sustain it. For it requires that we take the chances of freedom; that the liberating play of reason be brought to bear on events filled with passion; that dissent be allowed to make its appeal for acceptance; that men chance error in their search for the truth.

ROBERT F. KENNEDY, FORMER ATTORNEY GENERAL AND U.S. SENATOR

Our democracy is a fragile institution. Unless all the people are involved, the law is weakened. If people are left out, if they can't get jobs, if they can't get their civil rights restored, they become angry and alienated, and we are weaker and lower for it.

JANET RENO, FORMER U.S. ATTORNEY GENERAL

The great virtue of a free market system is that it does not care what color people are; it does not care what their religion is; it only cares whether they can produce something you want to buy. It is the most effective system we have discovered to enable people who hate one another to deal with one another and help one another.

MILTON FRIEDMAN, NOBEL PRIZE-WINNING ECONOMIST

One has the right to be wrong in a democracy.

CLAUDE PEPPER, FORMER U.S. SENATOR

The Ship of Democracy, which has weathered all storms, may sink through the mutiny of those on board.

GROVER CLEVELAND, 22ND PRESIDENT (1885–1889) AND 24TH PRESIDENT (1893–1897)

One of the strengths of democracy is the ability of the people to regularly demand changes in leadership and to fire a failing leader and hire a new one with the promise of hopeful change.

AL GORE, 45TH VICE PRESIDENT (1993–2001)

....

I believe in Democracy because it releases the energies of every human being.

WOODROW WILSON, 28TH PRESIDENT (1913–1921)

....

The preservation of the sacred fire of liberty and the destiny of the republican model of government are justly considered, perhaps, as deeply, as finally staked on the experiment entrusted to the hands of the American people.

GEORGE WASHINGTON, 1ST PRESIDENT (1789–1797)

The experience of democracy is like the experience of life itself—always changing, infinite in its variety, sometimes turbulent, and all the more valuable for having been tested by adversity.

JIMMY CARTER, 39TH PRESIDENT (1977–1981)

Democracy is not a fragile flower. Still it needs cultivating. If the rest of this century is to witness the gradual growth of freedom and democratic ideals, we must take actions to assist the campaign for democracy.

RONALD REAGAN, 40TH PRESIDENT (1981–1989)

All authority belongs to the people.

THOMAS JEFFERSON, 3RD PRESIDENT (1801–1809)

Human imperfections do not discredit democratic ideals. They make them more precious.

CONDOLEEZZA RICE, SECRETARY OF STATE AND FORMER NATIONAL SECURITY ADVISOR

In a free and republican government, you cannot restrain the voice of the multitude.

GEORGE WASHINGTON, 1ST PRESIDENT (1789–1797)

Where the people possess no authority, their rights obtain no respect.

GEORGE BANCROFT, HISTORIAN AND STATESMAN

Grassroots is the source of power. With it, you can do anything—without it, nothing.

GAYLORD NELSON, FORMER U.S. SENATOR

DISSENT

Those who make peaceful revolution impossible will make violent revolution inevitable.

    JOHN F. KENNEDY, 35TH PRESIDENT (1961–1963)

Freedom means the right of people to assemble, organize and debate openly. It means respecting the views of those who may disagree with the views of their governments. It means not taking citizens away from their loved ones and jailing they, mistreating them, or denying them their freedom or dignity because of the peaceful expression of their ideas and opinions.

    HILLARY RODHAM CLINTON, U.S. SENATOR AND FORMER FIRST LADY

Be careful not to assist in lighting a fire which you will have no ability to put out.

    BOOKER T. WASHINGTON, EDUCATOR AND CIVIL RIGHTS REFORMER

Honest and patriotic Americans have reached different conclusions as to how peace should be achieved. ... One of the strengths of our free society is that any American has a right to reach that conclusion and to advocate that point of view.

    RICHARD M. NIXON, 37TH PRESIDENT (1969–1974)

A free society is one where it is safe to be unpopular.

ADLAI STEVENSON, FORMER GOVERNOR OF ILLINOIS AND DIPLOMAT

Some boast of being friends to the government; I am a friend to righteous government, to a government founded upon the principles of reason and justice; but I glory in publicly avowing my eternal enmity to tyranny.

JOHN HANCOCK, AMERICAN REVOLUTIONARY LEADER

The only obligation which I have a right to assume is to do at any time what I think right.

HENRY DAVID THOREAU, ESSAYIST

When we are debating an issue, loyalty means giving me your honest opinion, whether you think I'll like it or not. Disagreement, at this stage, stimulates me. But once a decision has been made, the debate ends. From that point on, loyalty means executing the decision as if it were your own.

COLIN POWELL, FORMER SECRETARY OF STATE

....

The sharpest criticism often goes hand in hand with the deepest idealism and love of country.

ROBERT F. KENNEDY, FORMER ATTORNEY GENERAL

The spirit of resistance to government is so valuable on certain occasions that I wish it to be always kept alive. It will often be exercised when wrong, but better so than not to be exercised at all. I like a little rebellion now and then.

THOMAS JEFFERSON, 3RD PRESIDENT (1801–1809)

You're not supposed to be so blind with patriotism that you can't face reality. Wrong is wrong, no matter who says it.

MALCOLM X, MUSLIM LEADER

Moral cowardice that keeps us from speaking our minds is as dangerous to this country as irresponsible talk. The right way is not always the popular and easy way. Standing for right when it is unpopular is a true test of moral character.

MARGARET CHASE SMITH, FORMER U.S. REPRESENTATIVE AND U.S. SENATOR

So that this nation may long endure, I urge you to follow in the hallowed footsteps of the great disobediences of history that freed exiles, founded religions, defeated tyrants, and yes, in the hands of an aroused rabble in arms and a few great men, by God's grace, built this country.

CHARLTON HESTON, ACADEMY AWARD–WINNING ACTOR

Question everything. Every stripe, every star, every word spoken. Everything.

ERNEST J. GAINES, AUTHOR

You don't do anything automatically, simply because some "authority" (including me) says you should.

ISAAC ASIMOV, AUTHOR

Since the beginning of time, governments have been mainly engaged in kicking people around. The astonishing achievement in modern times in the Western world is the idea that the citizen should do the kicking.

ADLAI STEVENSON, FORMER GOVERNOR OF ILLINOIS AND DIPLOMAT

....

We must not confuse dissent with disloyalty.

EDWARD R. MURROW, RADIO AND TELEVISION BROADCASTER

....

Here in America we are descended in blood and in spirit from revolutionists and rebels—men and women who dare to dissent from accepted doctrine. As their heirs, may we never confuse honest dissent with disloyal subversion.

DWIGHT D. EISENHOWER, 34TH PRESIDENT (1953–1961)

If we don't believe in freedom of expression for people we despise, we don't believe in it at all.

NOAM CHOMSKY, LINGUIST AND POLITICAL ACTIVIST

In time of war even more than in time of peace, whether citizens happen to agree with the ruling administration or not, these precious fundamental personal rights—free speech, free press, and right of assemblage so explicitly and emphatically guaranteed by the Constitution—should be maintained inviolable.

ROBERT "FIGHTIN' BOB" LAFOLLETTE, FORMER U.S. SENATOR

The unity of freedom has never relied on uniformity of opinion.
> JOHN F. KENNEDY, 35TH PRESIDENT (1961–1963)

To announce that there must be no criticism of the President, or that we are to stand by the President, right or wrong, is not only unpatriotic and servile, but is morally treasonable to the American public.
> THEODORE ROOSEVELT, 26TH PRESIDENT (1901–1909)

Freedom is hammered out on the anvil of discussion, dissent, and debate.
> HUBERT HUMPHREY, 38TH VICE PRESIDENT (1965–1969)

The one thing that doesn't abide by majority rule is a person's conscience.
> HARPER LEE, PULITZER PRIZE-WINNING AUTHOR

....

If everyone is thinking alike then somebody isn't thinking.

GENERAL GEORGE S. PATTON

....

I would rather a thousand times be a free soul in jail than to be a sycophant and coward in the streets.
> EUGENE DEBS, LABOR ORGANIZER AND FOUNDER OF THE U.S. SOCIALIST PARTY

DUTY

—★—

A sense of honor and duty, a regard for the dignity of others as well as our own, and the shame we feel when we neglect them motivate both moral and physical courage.

JOHN McCAIN, U.S. SENATOR

There is only one basic human right, the right to do as you please. And with it comes the only basic human duty, the duty to take the consequences.

P.J. O'ROURKE, AUTHOR AND POLITICAL COMMENTATOR

It is the individual who can bring a tear to my eye and cause me to take a pen in my hand. It is the individual who has acted or tried to act, who will not only force a decision but have a hand in shaping it.

SANDRA DAY O'CONNOR, U.S. SUPREME COURT ASSOCIATE JUSTICE

Never allow it to be said that you are silent onlookers, detached spectators, but that you are involved participants in the struggle to make justice a reality.

MARTIN LUTHER KING, JR., CIVIL RIGHTS LEADER

None of us are self-made—and all of us owe a debt.

J.C. WATTS, FORMER U.S. REPRESENTATIVE

There is a mysterious cycle in human events. To some generations much is given. Of other generations much is expected.

FRANKLIN DELANO ROOSEVELT, 32ND PRESIDENT (1933–1945)

Duty is the sublimest word in our language. Do your duty in all things. You cannot do more. You should never wish to do less.

ROBERT E. LEE, CONFEDERATE GENERAL

There is no question what the roll of honor in America is. The roll of honor consists of the names of men who have squared their conduct by ideals of duty.

WOODROW WILSON, 28TH PRESIDENT (1913–1921)

....

A sense of duty is moral glue, constantly subject to stress.

WILLIAM SAFIRE, PULITZER PRIZE-WINNING JOURNALIST

....

My fellow citizens, each one of you carries on your shoulders not only the burden of doing well for the sake of your own country, but the burden of doing well and of seeing that this nation does well and of seeing that this nation does well for the sake of mankind.

THEODORE ROOSEVELT, 26TH PRESIDENT (1901–1909)

EDUCATION

───────★───────

To furnish the means of acquiring knowledge is ... the greatest benefit that can be conferred upon mankind.

JOHN QUINCY ADAMS, 6TH PRESIDENT (1825–1829)

The quality of strength lined with tenderness is an unbeatable combination, as are intelligence and necessity when unblunted by formal education.

MAYA ANGELOU, POET AND WRITER

The most important aspect of freedom of speech is freedom to learn. All education is a continuous dialogue—questions and answers that pursue every problem on the horizon. That is the essence of academic freedom.

WILLIAM O. DOUGLAS, FORMER U.S. SUPREME COURT ASSOCIATE JUSTICE

Learning is not attained by chance. It must be sought for with ardor and attended to with diligence.

ABIGAIL ADAMS, FORMER FIRST LADY

Books are the quietest and most constant of friends ... and the most patient of teachers.

CHARLES W. ELIOT, EDUCATOR

Being ignorant is not so much a shame as being unwilling to learn.

BENJAMIN FRANKLIN, STATESMAN AND SCIENTIST

The things taught in schools and colleges are not an education, but the means of education.

RALPH WALDO EMERSON, POET AND ESSAYIST

A little learning, indeed, may be a dangerous thing, but the want of learning is a calamity to any people.

FREDERICK DOUGLASS, ABOLITIONIST AND AUTOBIOGRAPHER

....

A person does not become educated because he is taught but because he is given a desire to learn.

BOB HOPE, ENTERTAINER

....

Books must be read as deliberately as they are written.

HENRY DAVID THOREAU, ESSAYIST

In a free world, if it is to remain free, we must maintain, with our lives if need be, but surely by our lives, the opportunity for a man to learn anything.

J. ROBERT OPPENHEIMER, PHYSICIST

Next in importance to freedom and justice is popular education, without which neither freedom nor justice can be permanently maintained.

JAMES GARFIELD, 20TH PRESIDENT (1881)

....

We are all born ignorant, but one must work hard to remain stupid.

BENJAMIN FRANKLIN, STATESMAN AND SCIENTIST

....

A child miseducated is a child lost.

JOHN F. KENNEDY, 35TH PRESIDENT (1961–1963)

Ignorance is of a peculiar nature; once dispelled, it is impossible to re-establish it. It is not originally a thing of itself, but is only the absence of knowledge; and though man may be kept ignorant, he cannot be made ignorant.

THOMAS PAINE, AMERICAN REVOLUTIONARY

We have an infinite amount to learn both from nature and from each other.

JOHN GLENN, FORMER SENATOR AND ASTRONAUT

Apply yourself. Get all the education you can, but then, by God, do something. Don't just stand there, make it happen.

LEE IACOCCA, AUTOMOBILE EXECUTIVE

Enlighten the people generally, and tyranny and oppressions of body and mind will vanish like evil spirits at the dawn of day.

THOMAS JEFFERSON, 3RD PRESIDENT (1801–1809)

Anyone who stops learning is old, whether at twenty or eighty. Anyone who keeps learning stays young. The greatest thing in life is to keep your mind young.

HENRY FORD, INDUSTRIALIST AND AUTOMOBILE MANUFACTURER

Nothing in the world is more dangerous than sincere ignorance and conscientious stupidity.

MARTIN LUTHER KING, JR., CIVIL RIGHTS LEADER

Every young man receives two educations—the first from his teachers; the second more personal and important, from himself.

BOB HOPE, ENTERTAINER

The advancement and diffusion of knowledge is the only guardian of true liberty.

JAMES MADISON, 4TH PRESIDENT (1809–1817)

Upon the subject of education, not presuming to dictate any plan or system respecting it, I can only say that I view it as the most important subject which we as a people may be engaged in. That everyone may receive at least a moderate education appears to be an objective of vital importance.

ABRAHAM LINCOLN, 16TH PRESIDENT (1861–1865)

Books were my pass to personal freedom. I learned to read at age three, and soon discovered there was a whole world to conquer that went beyond our farm in Mississippi.

OPRAH WINFREY, TELEVISION TALK-SHOW HOST, ACTRESS, AND PRODUCER

Some books leave us free and some books make us free.

RALPH WALDO EMERSON, POET AND ESSAYIST

Let us think of education as the means of developing our greatest abilities, because in each of us there is a private hope and dream which, fulfilled, can be translated into benefit for everyone and greater strength for our nation.

JOHN F. KENNEDY, 35TH PRESIDENT (1961–1963)

If a nation expects to be ignorant and free, in a state of civilization, it expects what never was and never will be.

THOMAS JEFFERSON, 3RD PRESIDENT (1801–1809)

Knowledge will forever govern ignorance; and a people who mean to be their own governors must arm themselves with the power which knowledge gives.

JAMES MADISON, 4TH PRESIDENT (1809–1817)

We are now at a point where we must educate our children in what no one knew yesterday, and prepare our schools for what no one knows yet.

MARGARET MEAD, ANTHROPOLOGIST

I have come to believe that a great teacher is a great artist and that there are as few as there are any other great artists. Teaching might even be the greatest of the arts since the medium is the human mind and spirit.

JOHN STEINBECK, NOBEL PRIZE-WINNING AUTHOR

If a man empties his purse into his head, no one can take it away from him. An investment of knowledge always pays the best interest.

BENJAMIN FRANKLIN, STATESMAN AND SCIENTIST

A democratic form of government, a democratic way of life, presupposed free public education over a long period; it presupposes also an education for personal responsibility that too often is neglected.

ELEANOR ROOSEVELT, FORMER FIRST LADY AND UNITED NATIONS DELEGATE

Education is our passport to the future, for tomorrow belongs to the people who prepare for it today.

MALCOLM X, MUSLIM LEADER

On the diffusion of education among the people rest the preservation and perpetuation of our free institutions.

DANIEL WEBSTER, STATESMAN AND LAWYER

Let us by all wise and constitutional measures promote intelligence among the people as the best means of preserving our liberties.

JAMES MONROE, 5TH PRESIDENT (1817–1825)

Education: That which reveals to the wise, and conceals from the stupid, the vast limits of their knowledge.

MARK TWAIN, AUTHOR AND HUMORIST

Educate and inform the whole mass of the people. ... They are the only sure reliance for the preservation of our liberty.

THOMAS JEFFERSON, 3RD PRESIDENT (1801–1809)

Intelligence plus character—that is the goal of true education.

MARTIN LUTHER KING, JR., CIVIL RIGHTS LEADER

The philosophy of the school room in one generation will be the philosophy of government in the next.

ABRAHAM LINCOLN, 16TH PRESIDENT (1861–1865)

Elections

—⭐—

A man without a vote is man without protection.
LYNDON B. JOHNSON, 36TH PRESIDENT (1963–1969)

In an American election, there are no losers, because whether or not our
candidates are successful, the next morning, we all wake up as Americans.
And that—that is the greatest privilege and the most remarkable good for-
tune that can come to us on Earth.
JOHN KERRY, U.S. SENATOR

We observe today not a victory of party but a celebration of freedom—sym-
bolizing an end as well as a beginning—signifying renewal as well as change.
JOHN F. KENNEDY, 35TH PRESIDENT (1961–1963)

The man who can right himself by a vote will seldom resort to a musket.
JAMES FENNIMORE COOPER, NOVELIST

It is more than appropriate, it is necessary that even in times of crisis we have
these contests, and engage in spirited disagreement over the shape and course
of our government. We have nothing to fear from each other.
JOHN MCCAIN, U.S. SENATOR

No man is worth his salt in public life who makes on the stump a pledge which he does not keep after election; and, if he makes such a pledge and does not keep it, hunt him out of public life.

THEODORE ROOSEVELT, 26TH PRESIDENT (1901–1909)

The ballot is stronger than the bullet.

ABRAHAM LINCOLN, 16TH PRESIDENT (1861–1865)

The vote is the most powerful instrument ever devised by man for breaking down injustice and destroying the terrible walls which imprison men because they are different from other men.

LYNDON B. JOHNSON, 36TH PRESIDENT (1963–1969)

....

We, the people, are the boss, and we will get the kind of political leadership, be it good or bad, that we demand and deserve.

JOHN F. KENNEDY, 35TH PRESIDENT (1961–1963)

....

It is in the nature of election campaigns to siphon off the vitality of people imbued with a heartfelt cause, dilute that cause, and pour it into the dubious endeavor to propel one somewhat better candidate into office.

HOWARD ZINN, HISTORIAN AND AUTHOR

Always vote for principle, though you may vote alone, and you may cherish the sweetest reflection that your vote is never lost.

JOHN QUINCY ADAMS, 6TH PRESIDENT (1825–1829)

The ballot box is the surest arbiter of disputes among free men.

JAMES BUCHANAN, 15TH PRESIDENT (1857–1861)

People tend to vote the present tense—not the subjective.

DIANE SAWYER, NEWS ANCHOR AND REPORTER

A democratic system where there is supposed to be noise, where there is supposed to be the clash of ideas and personalities, where the two candidates are doing it for one single purpose, not just to gain an office, but to find out what the American people want; to draw from them their hopes and dreams; to gain from the American people inspiration as to how they wish to be led.

COLIN POWELL, FORMER SECRETARY OF STATE

When annual elections end, there slavery begins.

JOHN ADAMS, 1ST VICE PRESIDENT (1789–1797) AND 2ND PRESIDENT (1797–1801)

If we do justice at the polls to our own conscience and sense of responsibility, then alone can we do justice to the nation we love; then alone can we make our beloved land a symbol and shrine of hope and faith for all free men.

ADLAI STEVENSON, FORMER GOVERNOR OF ILLINOIS AND DIPLOMAT

EQUALITY FOR WOMEN

We must strive to ensure that from the smallest village to the largest city, the vital voices of women will be heard at the ballot box and in legislatures, in classrooms and boardrooms, in counseling peace and building prosperity.

MADELEINE ALBRIGHT, FORMER SECRETARY OF STATE

Men their rights and nothing more; women their rights and nothing less.

SUSAN B. ANTHONY, FOUNDER OF THE NATIONAL WOMAN SUFFRAGE ASSOCIATION

It took 72 years of organized struggle on the part of many courageous women and men. It was one of America's most divisive philosophical wars. But it was also a bloodless war. Suffrage was achieved without a shot being fired.

HILLARY RODHAM CLINTON, U.S. SENATOR AND FORMER FIRST LADY

Since this society has been organized and so much thought and reading directed to the early struggles of this country, it has been made plain that much of its success was due to ... women of that era. The unselfish part they acted constantly commands itself to our admiration and example. If there is no abatement in this element of success in our ranks, I feel sure that their daughters can perpetuate a society worthy the cause and worthy themselves.

CAROLINE HARRISON, FORMER FIRST LADY

The struggle for equal opportunity in America is the struggle for America's soul. The ugliness of bigotry stands in direct contradiction to the very meaning of America.

HUBERT HUMPHREY, 38TH VICE PRESIDENT (1965–1969)

We, all of us, should think very much more carefully than we do about what we mean by freedom of speech, by freedom of the press, by freedom of assembly. ... Some people seem to think these rights are not for people who disagree with them.

ELEANOR ROOSEVELT, FORMER FIRST LADY AND UNITED NATIONS DELEGATE

....

Every time we liberate a woman, we liberate a man.

MARGARET MEAD, ANTHROPOLOGIST

....

By choosing a woman to run for our nation's second highest office, you send a powerful signal to all Americans: There are no doors we cannot unlock. We will place no limits on achievement. If we can do this, we can do anything.

GERALDINE FERRARO, 1984 DEMOCRATIC VICE PRESIDENTIAL NOMINEE

If women's suffrage is wrong, it is a great wrong; if it is right, it is a profound and fundamental principle ... upon which a republic must rise.

ANNA HOWARD SHAW, SUFFRAGIST LEADER

No country or culture has a monopoly on what is right for a woman to think or believe. Our goal is to help women everywhere to express themselves.

MADELEINE ALBRIGHT, FORMER SECRETARY OF STATE

....

Freedom and equality for all depend first on whether a citizen truly has a voice.

HILLARY RODHAM CLINTON, U.S. SENATOR

....

Men and women must go through this world together from the cradle to the grave; it is God's way, and it is the fundamental principle of a republican form of government.

ANNA HOWARD SHAW, SUFFRAGIST LEADER

I never doubted that equal rights was the right direction. Most reforms, most problems are complicated. But to me there is nothing complicated about ordinary equality.

ALICE PAUL, WOMEN'S SUFFRAGE LEADER

The minute we deny any rights of this kind to any citizen, we are preparing the way for the denial of those rights to someone else.

ELEANOR ROOSEVELT, FORMER FIRST LADY AND UNITED NATIONS DELEGATE

My idea about higher culture for women is that it makes them great in intellect and soul, develops the lofty conception of womanhood; not that it makes them a poor imitation of a man ... woman is the complement of man. ... No fundamental superiority or inferiority between the two appears plain to me.

HELEN TAFT, FORMER FIRST LADY

I think, with never-ending gratitude, that the young women of today do not and can never know at what price their right to free speech and to speak at all in public has been earned.

LUCY STONE, WOMEN'S SUFFRAGE LEADER

If we are to achieve a richer culture, rich in contrasting values, we must recognize the whole gamut of human potentialities, and so weave a less arbitrary social fabric, one in which each diverse human gift will find a fitting place.

MARGARET MEAD, ANTHROPOLOGIST

....

Whatever the theories may be of woman's dependence on man, in the supreme moments of her life he can not bear her burdens.

ELIZABETH CADY STANTON, WOMEN'S SUFFRAGE LEADER

FAITH

---★---

God is interested in the freedom of the whole human race, the creation of a society where every man will respect the dignity and worth of personality.

MARTIN LUTHER KING, JR., CIVIL RIGHTS LEADER

It is only when men begin to worship that they begin to grow.

CALVIN COOLIDGE, 30TH PRESIDENT (1923–1929)

What greater calamity can fall upon a nation than the loss of worship? Then all things go to decay.

RALPH WALDO EMERSON, POET AND ESSAYIST

When religion begins to take part in politics, we violate something which we have set up, which is a division between church and state.

ELEANOR ROOSEVELT, FORMER FIRST LADY AND UNITED NATIONS DELEGATE

I don't want to claim that God is on our side. As Abraham Lincoln told us, I want to pray humbly that we are on God's side. And whatever our faith, one belief should bind us all: The measure of our character is our willingness to give of ourselves for others and for our country.

JOHN KERRY, U.S. SENATOR

I believe that if we really want human brotherhood to spread and increase until it makes life safe and sane, we must also be certain that there is no one true faith or path by which it may spread.

ADLAI STEVENSON, FORMER GOVERNOR OF ILLINOIS AND DIPLOMAT

We must never judge the fitness of individuals to govern on the bas[is] of where they worship, whether they follow Christ or Moses, whether they are called "born again" or "ungodly."

EDWARD M. KENNEDY, U.S. SENATOR

A prayerful spirit has always been a central part of our national tradition, and it remains a vital part of our national character.

GEORGE W. BUSH, 43RD PRESIDENT (2001–)

Tell the truth, have you ever found God in a church? I never did. I just found a bunch of folks hoping for him to show. Any God I ever felt in church I brought in with me. And I think all the other folks did too. They come to church to share God, not find God.

ALICE WALKER, AUTHOR

Faith is taking the first step even when you don't see the whole staircase.

MARTIN LUTHER KING, JR., CIVIL RIGHTS LEADER

....

Americans do not presume to equate God's purposes with any purpose of our own. God's will is greater than any man, or any nation built by men.

GEORGE W. BUSH, 43RD PRESIDENT (2001–   )

But let not the foundation of our hope rest upon man's wisdom. It will not be sufficient that sectional prejudices find no place in the public deliberations. It will not be sufficient that the rash counsels of human passion are rejected. It must be felt that there is no national security but in the nation's humble, acknowledged dependence upon God and His overruling providence.

FRANKLIN PIERCE, 14TH PRESIDENT (1853–1857)

Faith is much better than belief. Belief is when someone else does the thinking.

R. BUCKMINSTER FULLER, ARCHITECT AND ENGINEER

Prayer does not use up artificial energy, doesn't burn up any fossil fuel, doesn't pollute. Neither does song, neither does love, neither does the dance.

MARGARET MEAD, ANTHROPOLOGIST

This nation was not founded on the belief that if one just cares about himself enough ... everything will be fine. It was founded on an idea of justice which acknowledged that the source of human dignity and human rights and human hope was not the decision and will of human beings, but the power and will of Almighty God, the Creator.

ALAN KEYES, FORMER U.S. REPRESENTATIVE TO THE UNITED NATIONS

I hope for an America where neither "fundamentalist" nor "humanist" will be a dirty word, but a fair description of the different ways in which people of good will look at life and into their own souls.

EDWARD M. KENNEDY, U.S. SENATOR

Parchment will fail, the sword will fail, it is only the spiritual nature of man that can be triumphant.

CALVIN COOLIDGE, 30TH PRESIDENT (1923–1929)

Freedom

———— ★ ————

The mind of America must be forever free.

CALVIN COOLIDGE, 30TH PRESIDENT (1923–1929)

The proper response to difficulty is not to retreat; it is to prevail. The advance of freedom always carries a cost, paid by the bravest among us.

GEORGE W. BUSH, 43RD PRESIDENT (2001–)

Eternal vigilance is the price of liberty.

THOMAS JEFFERSON, 3RD PRESIDENT (1801–1809)

Knowing the difficulties of America's own history, we should always be humble in singing freedom's praises. But America's voice should never waver in speaking out on the side of people seeking freedom.

CONDOLEEZZA RICE, SECRETARY OF STATE AND FORMER NATIONAL SECURITY ADVISOR

Does there exist a nobler inspiration than the desire to be free? It is by his freedom that a man knows himself, by his sovereignty over his own life. To violate freedom, to flout that sovereignty, is to deny man the right to live his life, to take responsibility for himself with dignity.

ELIE WIESEL, AUTHOR AND NOBEL PEACE PRIZE WINNER

The cost of freedom is always high—but Americans have always paid it. And one path we shall never choose, and that is the path of surrender or submission.

JOHN F. KENNEDY, 35TH PRESIDENT (1961–1963)

Once you give people freedom, they don't willingly give it up. And we have had freedom for a long time, and I think the mission of this country is to try to share it with others, because we realize the more people who live in freedom, the more peaceful the world is going to be.

RUDOLPH GIULIANI, FORMER MAYOR OF NEW YORK CITY

The shallow consider liberty a release from all law, from every constraint. The wise see in it, on the contrary, the potent Law of Laws.

WALT WHITMAN, POET AND ESSAYIST

What is freedom? Freedom is the right to choose; the right to create for oneself the alternatives of choice. Without the possibility of choice and the exercise of choice a man is not a man but a member, an instrument, a thing.

ARCHIBALD MACLEISH, PULITZER PRIZE-WINNING PLAYWRIGHT

....

Where liberty dwells, there is my country.

BENJAMIN FRANKLIN, STATESMAN AND SCIENTIST

....

The defense of freedom is everybody's business—not just America's business.

RICHARD M. NIXON, 37TH PRESIDENT (1969–1974)

He that would make his own liberty secure must guard even his enemy from oppression.

THOMAS PAINE, AMERICAN REVOLUTIONARY

....

At times history and fate meet at a single time in a single place to shape a turning point in man's unending search for freedom.

LYNDON B. JOHNSON, 36TH PRESIDENT (1963–1969)

....

For what avail the plough or sail, Or land or life, if freedom fail?

RALPH WALDO EMERSON, POET AND ESSAYIST

Liberty—liberty within the law—and civilization are inseparable ... and there comes to Americans the profound assurance that our representative government is the highest expression and surest guaranty of both.

WARREN G. HARDING, 29TH PRESIDENT (1921–1923)

That very word freedom, in itself and of necessity, suggests freedom from some restraining power.

FRANKLIN DELANO ROOSEVELT, 32ND PRESIDENT (1933–1945)

Never make the mistake of assuming that some people do not share your desire to live freely, to think and believe as you would like to see fit, to raise a family and educate children, boys and girls. Never make the mistake of assuming that some people do not desire the freedom to chart their own course in life.

CONDOLEEZZA RICE, SECRETARY OF STATE AND FORMER NATIONAL SECURITY ADVISOR

Only free peoples can hold their purpose and their honor steady to a common end and prefer the interests of mankind to any narrow interest of their own.

WOODROW WILSON, 28TH PRESIDENT (1913–1921)

Perfect freedom is as necessary to the health and vigor of commerce as it is to the health and vigor of citizenship.

PATRICK HENRY, AMERICAN REVOLUTIONARY LEADER

I leave you, hoping that the lamp of liberty will burn in your bosoms, until there shall no longer be a doubt that all men are created free and equal.

ABRAHAM LINCOLN, 16TH PRESIDENT (1861–1865)

I have sworn upon the altar of God, eternal hostility against every form of tyranny over the mind of man.

THOMAS JEFFERSON, 3RD PRESIDENT (1801–1809)

Freedom is not an unlimited license, an unlimited choice, or an unlimited opportunity. Freedom is first of all a responsibility before the God from whom we come.

ALAN KEYES, FORMER U.S. REPRESENTATIVE TO THE UNITED NATIONS

We must be staunch in our conviction that freedom is not the sole prerogative of a lucky few, but the inalienable and universal right of all human beings.

RONALD REAGAN, 40TH PRESIDENT (1981—1989)

Man is man because he is free to operate within the framework of his destiny. He is free to deliberate, to make decisions, and to choose between alternatives. He is distinguished from animals by his freedom to do evil or to do good and to walk the high road of beauty or tread the low road of ugly degeneracy.

MARTIN LUTHER KING, JR., CIVIL RIGHTS LEADER

....

God grants liberty only to those who love it, and are always ready to guard and defend it.

DANIEL WEBSTER, STATESMAN AND LAWYER

....

If you're not ready to die for it, put the word "freedom" out of your vocabulary.

MALCOLM X, MUSLIM LEADER

When freedom is being sought by brave people living under tyranny, we must stand on their side. And when newly free people are seeking to build the institutions of law and democracy, we have an obligation if asked to help.

CONDOLEEZZA RICE, SECRETARY OF STATE AND FORMER NATIONAL SECURITY ADVISOR

Freedom is no half-and-half affair.

FRANKLIN DELANO ROOSEVELT, 32ND PRESIDENT (1933–1945)

....

We must rededicate ourselves to completing the circle of human rights once and for all. We must challenge ourselves to see more sharply, to hear more clearly, to feel more fully.

HILLARY RODHAM CLINTON, U.S. SENATOR AND FORMER FIRST LADY

The greatest dangers to liberty lurk in insidious encroachment by men of zeal, well-meaning but without understanding.

LOUIS BRANDEIS, FORMER U.S. SUPREME COURT ASSOCIATE JUSTICE

We cannot choose freedom established on a hierarchy of degrees of freedom, on a caste system of equality like military rank. We must be free not because we claim freedom, but because we practice it.

WILLIAM FAULKNER, NOBEL PRIZE-WINNING AUTHOR

Order without liberty and liberty without order are equally destructive.

THEODORE ROOSEVELT, 26TH PRESIDENT (1901–1909)

Volumes can be and have been written about the issue of freedom versus dictatorship, but, in essence, it comes down to a single question: Do you consider it moral to treat men as sacrificial animals and to rule them by physical force?

AYN RAND, AUTHOR

[The people] are the only sure reliance for the preservation of our liberty.

THOMAS JEFFERSON, 3RD PRESIDENT (1801–1809)

Liberty, according to my metaphysics, is a self-determining power in an intellectual agent. It implies thought and choice and power.

JOHN ADAMS, 1ST VICE PRESIDENT (1789–1797) AND 2ND PRESIDENT (1797–1801)

A free America ... means just this: Individual freedom for all, rich or poor, or else this system of government we call democracy is only an expedient to enslave man to the machine and make him like it.

FRANK LLOYD WRIGHT, ARCHITECT

Freedom and the dignity of the individual have been more available and assured here than in any other place on Earth. The price for this freedom at times has been high, but we have been unwilling to pay that price.

RONALD REAGAN, 40TH PRESIDENT (1981–1989)

....

The liberty we cherish, and in which we want all people to share, has a price.

JOHN MCCAIN, U.S. SENATOR

....

It is harder to preserve than obtain liberty.

JOHN C. CALHOUN, 7TH VICE PRESIDENT

I looked at my hands, to see if I was the same person now I was free. There was such a glory over everything, the sun came like gold through the trees, and over the fields, and I felt like I was in heaven.

HARRIET TUBMAN, ABOLITIONIST

....

Everything that is really great and inspiring is created by the individual who can labor in freedom.

ALBERT EINSTEIN, NOBEL PRIZE-WINNING PHYSICIST

....

Freedom means the supremacy of human rights everywhere.

FRANKLIN DELANO ROOSEVELT, 32ND PRESIDENT (1933–1945)

No man who knows ought, can be so stupid to deny that all men naturally were born free.

EDWARD R. MURROW, RADIO AND TELEVISION BROADCASTER

Liberty lies in the hearts of men and women; when it dies there, no constitution, no law, no court can save it; no constitution, no law, no court can even do much to help it. While it lies there it needs no constitution, no law, no court to save it.

LEARNED HAND, JURIST

Our defense is in the preservation of the spirit which prizes liberty as a heritage of all men, in all lands, everywhere. Destroy this spirit and you have planted the seeds of despotism around your own doors.

ABRAHAM LINCOLN, 16TH PRESIDENT (1861–1865)

Those who expect to reap the blessings of freedom must, like men, undergo the fatigue of supporting it.

THOMAS PAINE, AMERICAN REVOLUTIONARY

Freedom, by its nature, must be chosen, and defended by citizens, and sustained by the rule of law and the protection of minorities.

GEORGE W. BUSH, 43RD PRESIDENT (2001–)

Posterity: You will never know how much it has cost my generation to preserve your freedom. I hope you will make good use of it.

JOHN QUINCY ADAMS, 6TH PRESIDENT (1825–1829)

Those who won our independence ... valued liberty as an end and as a means. They believed liberty to be the secret of happiness and courage to be the secret of liberty.

LOUIS BRANDEIS, FORMER U.S. SUPREME COURT ASSOCIATE JUSTICE

At the present moment in world history nearly every nation must choose between alternative ways of life. The choice is too often not a free one.

HARRY S. TRUMAN, 33RD PRESIDENT (1945–1953)

We, and all others who believe in freedom as deeply as we do, would rather die on our feet than live on our knees.

FRANKLIN DELANO ROOSEVELT, 32ND PRESIDENT (1933–1945)

It is my living sentiment, and by the blessing of God it shall be my dying sentiment—Independence now and Independence forever!

DANIEL WEBSTER, STATESMAN AND LAWYER

Military Power ... will never awe a sensible American tamely to surrender his liberty.

SAMUEL ADAMS, AMERICAN REVOLUTIONARY LEADER

Freedom is not an ideal, it is not even a protection, if it means nothing more than the freedom to stagnate.

ADLAI STEVENSON, FORMER GOVERNOR OF ILLINOIS AND DIPLOMAT

....

The future of liberty means the future of civilization.

HENRY HAZLITT, JOURNALIST AND ECONOMIST

You can't separate peace from freedom because no one can be at peace unless he has his freedom.

MALCOLM X, MUSLIM LEADER

The fundamental precept of liberty is toleration.

CALVIN COOLIDGE, 30TH PRESIDENT (1923–1929)

Knowing what we know about the difficulties of our own history, knowing the history of Alabama and Mississippi and Tennessee, we should be humble in singing freedom's praise, but our voice should never waiver in speaking out on the side of those who seek freedom.

CONDOLEEZZA RICE, SECRETARY OF STATE AND FORMER NATIONAL SECURITY ADVISOR

Liberty cannot be preserved without a general knowledge among the people.

JOHN ADAMS, 1ST VICE PRESIDENT (1789–1797) AND 2ND PRESIDENT (1797–1801)

Freedom is indivisible, and when one man is enslaved, all are not free.

JOHN F. KENNEDY, 35TH PRESIDENT (1961–1963)

The future belongs to those who dream the oldest and noblest dream of all: the dream of peace and freedom.

PAUL WOLFOWITZ, DEPUTY SECRETARY OF DEFENSE

Americans are a free people, who know that freedom is the right of every person and the future of every nation. The liberty we prize is not America's gift to the world; it is God's gift to humanity.

GEORGE W. BUSH, 43RD PRESIDENT (2001–   )

....

Liberty never dies.

HERALD ICKES, FORMER SECRETARY OF THE INTERIOR

....

Systems political or religious or racial or national—will not just respect us because we practice freedom, they will fear us because we do.

WILLIAM FAULKNER, NOBEL PRIZE-WINNING AUTHOR

Only our individual faith in freedom can keep us free.

DWIGHT D. EISENHOWER, 34TH PRESIDENT (1953–1961)

Guard with jealous attention the public liberty. Suspect everyone who approaches that jewel. Unfortunately, nothing will preserve it but downright force. Whenever you give up that force, you are inevitably ruined.

PATRICK HENRY, AMERICAN REVOLUTIONARY LEADER

We welcome change and openness; for we believe that freedom and security go together, that the advance of human liberty can only strengthen the cause of world peace.

RONALD REAGAN, 40TH PRESIDENT (1981–1989)

Liberty has never come from the government. Liberty has always come from the subjects of government. The history of liberty is the history of resistance. The history of liberty is a history of the limitation of governmental power, not the increase of it.

WOODROW WILSON, 28TH PRESIDENT (1913–1921)

....

It is easy to take liberty for granted when you have never had it taken from you.

DICK CHENEY, 46TH VICE PRESIDENT (2001–   )

....

All of us, despite the differences that enliven our politics, are united in the one big idea that freedom is our birthright and its defense is always our first responsibility. All other responsibilities come second.

JOHN MCCAIN, U.S. SENATOR

We fought, not for territory but for justice, not for plunder but to liberate peoples enslaved. We fought for the love of liberty, a faith that each generation must define, and sometimes defend, in its own way.

BOB DOLE, FORMER U.S. SENATE MAJORITY LEADER

Extremism in the defense of liberty is no vice! ... [M]oderation in the pursuit of justice is no virtue!

BARRY GOLDWATER, FORMER U.S. SENATOR

I would rather be exposed to the inconveniences attending too much liberty than those attending too small a degree of it.

THOMAS JEFFERSON, 3RD PRESIDENT (1801–1809)

History teaches that freedom must make its case, again and again, from one generation to the next. The work of freedom is never done.

ANTHONY M. KENNEDY, U.S. SUPREME COURT ASSOCIATE JUSTICE

Freedom has its life in the hearts, the actions, the spirit of men and so it must be daily earned and refreshed—else like a flower cut from its life—giving roots, it will wither and die.

DWIGHT D. EISENHOWER, 34TH PRESIDENT (1953–1961)

No power on earth has a right to take our property from us without our consent. Every fence that the wisdom of our British ancestors had carefully erected against arbitrary power has been violently thrown down.

JOHN JAY, FORMER U.S. SUPREME COURT CHIEF JUSTICE

Give me liberty or give me death.

PATRICK HENRY, AMERICAN REVOLUTIONARY LEADER

Freedom is never voluntarily given by the oppressor; it must be demanded by the oppressed.

MARTIN LUTHER KING, JR., CIVIL RIGHTS LEADER

Freedom is about authority. Freedom is about the willingness of every single human being to cede to lawful authority a great deal of discretion about what you do and how you do it.

RUDOLPH GIULIANI, FORMER MAYOR OF NEW YORK CITY

Freedom is never more than one generation away from extinction. We didn't pass it to our children in the bloodstream. It must be fought for, protected, and handed on for them to do the same, or one day we will spend our sunset years telling our children and our children's children what it was once like in the United States where men were free.

RONALD REAGAN, 40TH PRESIDENT (1981–1989)

I would rather belong to a poor nation that was free than to a rich nation that had ceased to be in love with liberty. We shall not be poor if we love liberty.

WOODROW WILSON, 28TH PRESIDENT (1913–1921)

....

Human kindness has never weakened the stamina or softened the fiber of a free people. A nation does not have to be cruel in order to be tough.

FRANKLIN DELANO ROOSEVELT, 32ND PRESIDENT (1933–1945)

Liberty is the only thing you cannot have unless you are willing to give it to others.

WILLIAM ALLEN WHITE, JOURNALIST AND AUTHOR

....

Liberty, when it begins to take root, is a plant of rapid growth.

GEORGE WASHINGTON, 1ST PRESIDENT (1789–1797)

....

I hope for an America where we can all contend freely and vigorously, but where we will treasure and guard those standards of civility which alone make this nation safe for both democracy and diversity.

EDWARD M. KENNEDY, U.S. SENATOR

Americans, of all people, should never be surprised by the power of our ideals. Eventually, the call of freedom comes to every mind and every soul. We do not accept the existence of permanent tyranny because we do not accept the possibility of permanent slavery. Liberty will come to those who love it.

GEORGE W. BUSH, 43RD PRESIDENT (2001–   )

We have to love our freedom, not just for the material benefits it provides, not just for the autonomy it guarantees us, but for the goodness it makes possible.

JOHN MCCAIN, U.S. SENATOR

We stand for freedom. That is our conviction for ourselves; that is our only commitment to others.

JOHN F. KENNEDY, 35TH PRESIDENT (1961–1963)

Individuality is freedom lived.

JOHN DOS PASSOS, AUTHOR

A country cannot subsist well without liberty, nor liberty without virtue.

DANIEL WEBSTER, STATESMAN AND LAWYER

....

The God who gave us life gave us liberty at the same time.

THOMAS JEFFERSON, 3RD PRESIDENT (1801–1809)

....

THE FUTURE

★

I must study politics and war that my sons may have liberty to study mathematics and philosophy.

JOHN ADAMS, 1ST VICE PRESIDENT (1789–1797) AND 2ND PRESIDENT (1797–1801)

If anyone tells you that America's best days are behind her, they're looking the wrong way.

GEORGE H.W. BUSH, 41ST PRESIDENT (1989–1993)

As we peer into society's future ... we must avoid the impulse to live only for today, plundering, for our own ease and convenience, the precious resources of tomorrow.

DWIGHT D. EISENHOWER, 34TH PRESIDENT (1953–1961)

The America we long for is still out there, somewhere ahead of us, waiting for us to find her.

JIMMY CARTER, 39TH PRESIDENT (1977–1981)

The future is not a gift; it is an achievement. Every generation helps make its own future. This is the essential challenge of the present.

ROBERT F. KENNEDY, FORMER ATTORNEY GENERAL AND U.S. SENATOR

I rely on history as my guide to the future, and history shows us, unequivocally, that this nation has stood for freedom and democracy, even at the risk and loss of American lives, so that all might enjoy the same privileges or have the opportunity to someday enjoy the same privileges as we do in this noble experiment called the United States of America.

JOHN McCAIN, U.S. SENATOR

We are the beneficiaries of the work of the generations before us, and it is each generation's responsibility to continue that work.

LAURA BUSH, FIRST LADY

I believe America's best days are ahead of us because I believe that the future belongs to freedom, not to fear.

JOHN KERRY, U.S. SENATOR

America is still the land of golden dreams, and it's the duty of our generation to make sure that our children and our children's children have all the opportunities that we have enjoyed—and more.

DICK CHENEY, 46TH VICE PRESIDENT (2001–   )

....

The future doesn't belong to the faint-hearted; it belongs to the brave.

RONALD REAGAN, 40TH PRESIDENT (1981–1989)

My best judgment of America's needs is to steady down, to get squarely on our feet, to make sure of the right path.

WARREN G. HARDING, 29TH PRESIDENT

Behind us we can look back and see the great expanse of American achievement; and before us we can see even greater, grander frontiers of possibility.

WILLIAM J. CLINTON, 42ND PRESIDENT (1993–2001)

I can conceive of a national destiny surpassing the glories of the present and the past—a destiny which meets the responsibility of today and measures up to the possibilities of the future.

WILLIAM JENNINGS BRYAN, STATESMAN

Let us be a concerned generation.

MARTIN LUTHER KING, JR., CIVIL RIGHTS LEADER

I see an America poised not only at the brink of a new century, but at the dawn of a new era of honest, compassionate, responsive government.

JIMMY CARTER, 39TH PRESIDENT (1977–1981)

If future generations are to remember us more with gratitude than sorrow, we must achieve more than just the miracles of technology. We must also leave them a glimpse of the world as it was created, not just as it looked when we got through with it.

LYNDON B. JOHNSON, 36TH PRESIDENT (1963–1969)

I like the dreams of the future better than the history of the past.

THOMAS JEFFERSON, 3RD PRESIDENT (1801–1809)

This tide of the future, the democratic future, is ours. It is ours if we show ourselves worthy of our culture and of our heritage.

HERALD ICKES, FORMER SECRETARY OF THE INTERIOR

Every age needs men who will redeem the time by living with a vision of the things that are to be.

ADLAI STEVENSON, FORMER GOVERNOR OF ILLINOIS

Our faith that we can shape a better future is what the American dream is all about. The promise of our country is that the rules are fair. If you work hard and play by the rules, you can earn your share of America's blessings.

GERALDINE FERRARO, 1984 DEMOCRATIC VICE PRESIDENTIAL NOMINEE

When we are planning for posterity, we ought to remember that virtue is not hereditary.

<small>THOMAS PAINE, AMERICAN REVOLUTIONARY</small>

....

It is the high privilege and sacred duty of those now living to educate their successors and fit them, by intelligence and virtue, for the inheritance which awaits them.

<small>JAMES GARFIELD, 20TH PRESIDENT (1881)</small>

Happy as our situation is, it does not exempt us from solicitude and care for the future. On the contrary, as the blessings which we enjoy are great, proportionably great should be our vigilance, zeal, and activity to preserve them.

<small>JAMES MONROE, 5TH PRESIDENT (1817–1825)</small>

Let us make America once again and for centuries more to come what it has so long been—a stronghold and a beacon-light of liberty for the whole world.

<small>GERALD R. FORD, 38TH PRESIDENT (1974–1977)</small>

I now begin the journey that will lead me into the sunset of my life. I know that for America there will always be a bright dawn ahead.

<small>RONALD REAGAN, 40TH PRESIDENT (1981–1989)</small>

The encouraging feature of our country is not that it has reached its destination, but that it has overwhelmingly expressed its determination to proceed in the right direction.

CALVIN COOLIDGE, 30TH PRESIDENT (1923–1929)

I look forward to a great future for America—a future in which our country will match its military strength with our moral restraint, its wealth with our wisdom, its power with our purpose.

JOHN F. KENNEDY, 35TH PRESIDENT (1961–1963)

You cannot escape the responsibility of tomorrow by evading it today.

ABRAHAM LINCOLN, 16TH PRESIDENT (1861–1865)

All great change in America begins at the dinner table. So, tomorrow night in the kitchen I hope the talking begins. And children, if your parents haven't been teaching you what it means to be an American, let 'em know and nail 'em on it. That would be a very American thing to do.

RONALD REAGAN, 40TH PRESIDENT (1981–1989)

....

All of you here today can be heroes of tomorrow—you can make a remarkable difference in this world.

JERRY MORAN, U.S. REPRESENTATIVE

In the years ahead, America will be called upon to demonstrate character, consistency, courage and leadership.

GENERAL TOMMY FRANKS

It is a new world, but America should not fear it.

JIMMY CARTER, 39TH PRESIDENT (1977–1981)

One faces the future with one's past.

PEARL S. BUCK, NOBEL PRIZE-WINNING AUTHOR

I never think of the future. It comes soon enough.

ALBERT EINSTEIN, NOBEL PRIZE-WINNING PHYSICIST

The future does not belong to those who are content with today, apathetic toward common problems and their fellow man alike, timid and fearful in the face of new ideas and bold projects. Rather it will belong to those who can blend vision, reason and courage in a personal commitment to the ideals and great enterprises of American Society.

ROBERT F. KENNEDY, FORMER ATTORNEY GENERAL AND U.S. SENATOR

GOVERNMENT

———⋆———

The foundation of every government is some principle or passion in the minds of the people. The noblest principles and most generous affections in our nature, then, have the fairest chance to support the noblest and most generous models of government.

JOHN ADAMS, 1ST VICE PRESIDENT (1789–1797) AND 2ND PRESIDENT (1797–1801)

Government can and must provide opportunity, not smother it; foster productivity, not stifle it.

RONALD REAGAN, 40TH PRESIDENT (1981–1989)

Some needs, government cannot fulfill: the need for kindness, and for understanding, and for love.

GEORGE W. BUSH, 43RD PRESIDENT (2001–   )

The object of government is the welfare of the people.

THEODORE ROOSEVELT, 26TH PRESIDENT (1901–1909)

The problems of maintained civilization are not to be solved by a transfer of responsibility from citizenship to government.

WARREN G. HARDING, 29TH PRESIDENT (1921–1923)

The only sure bulwark of continuing liberty is a government strong enough to protect the interests of the people, and a people strong enough and well enough informed to maintain its sovereign control over its government.

FRANKLIN DELANO ROOSEVELT, 32ND PRESIDENT (1933–1945)

All free governments are managed by the combined wisdom and folly of the people.

JAMES GARFIELD, 20TH PRESIDENT (1881)

Sometimes it is said that man can not be trusted with the government of himself. Can he, then, be trusted with the government of others? Or have we found angels in the forms of kings to govern him?

THOMAS JEFFERSON, 3RD PRESIDENT (1801–1809)

A simple and proper function of government is just to make it easy for us to do good and difficult for us to do wrong.

JIMMY CARTER, 39TH PRESIDENT (1977–1981)

....

Government is not reason; it is not eloquence; it is force! Like fire, it is a dangerous servant and a fearful master.

GEORGE WASHINGTON, 1ST PRESIDENT (1789–1797)

If the government becomes the lawbreaker, it breeds contempt for law; it invites every man to become a law unto himself; it invites anarchy.

LOUIS BRANDEIS, FORMER U.S. SUPREME COURT ASSOCIATE JUSTICE

Majority rule only works if you're also considering individual rights. Because you can't have five wolves and one sheep voting on what to have for supper.

LARRY FLYNT, PUBLISHER AND CIVIL RIGHTS ADVOCATE

....

When there is a lack of honor in government, the morals of the whole people are poisoned.

HERBERT HOOVER, 31ST PRESIDENT (1929–1933)

....

Throughout America's adventure in free government, our basic purposes have been to keep the peace; to foster progress in human achievement, and to enhance liberty, dignity and integrity among people and among nations. To strive for less would be unworthy of a free and religious people.

DWIGHT D. EISENHOWER, 34TH PRESIDENT (1953–1961)

If men were angels, no government would be necessary.

JAMES MADISON, 4TH PRESIDENT (1809–1817)

Government has no monopoly on compassion. Indeed, government is compassion's least able practitioner.

JERRY MORAN, U.S. REPRESENTATIVE

It is not the function of the government to keep the citizen from falling into error; it is the function of the citizen to keep the government from falling into error.

ROBERT H. JACKSON, FORMER U.S. SUPREME COURT ASSOCIATE JUSTICE

The efforts of the government alone will never be enough. In the end the people must choose and the people must help themselves.

JOHN F. KENNEDY, 35TH PRESIDENT (1961–1963)

The world needs to be reminded that all human ills are not curable by legislation, and that quantity of statutory enactment and excess of government offer no substitute for quality of citizenship.

WARREN G. HARDING, 29TH PRESIDENT (1921–1923)

The national government belongs to the whole American people, and where the whole American people are interested, that interest can be guarded effectively only by the national government.

THEODORE ROOSEVELT, 26TH PRESIDENT (1901–1909)

It is to be regretted that the right and powerful too often bend the acts of government to their selfish purposes.

ANDREW JACKSON, 7TH PRESIDENT (1829–1837)

The government is merely a servant—merely a temporary servant; it cannot be its prerogative to determine what is right and what is wrong, and decide who is a patriot and who isn't. Its function is to obey orders, not originate them.

MARK TWAIN, AUTHOR AND HUMORIST

The First Amendment protects religion from government, not government from religion.

REAR ADMIRAL JEREMIAH A. DENTON, FORMER U.S. SENATOR

[Government] cannot provide values to persons who have none, or who have lost those they had. It cannot provide inner peace. It can provide outlets for moral energies, but it cannot create those energies.

DANIEL PATRICK MOYNIHAN, FORMER U.S. SENATOR

A government that remembers that the people are its master is a good and needed thing.

GEORGE H.W. BUSH, 41ST PRESIDENT (1989–1993)

....

Every segment of our population, and every individual, has a right to expect from his government a fair deal.

HARRY S. TRUMAN, 33RD PRESIDENT (1945–1953)

The great essential to our happiness and prosperity is that we adhere to the principles upon which the Government was established and insist upon their faithful observance.

WILLIAM McKINLEY, 25TH PRESIDENT (1897–1901)

....

There are no necessary evils in government. Its evils exist only in its abuses.

ANDREW JACKSON, 7TH PRESIDENT (1829–1837)

....

The American government isn't contained within a specific building or setting. It's found in the commitment of the American people to our democratic principles.

TOM DELAY, MAJORITY LEADER OF THE U.S. HOUSE OF REPRESENTATIVES

A government can't control the economy without controlling people.

RONALD REAGAN, 40TH PRESIDENT (1981–1989)

Government cannot solve our problems, it can't set our goals, it cannot define our vision. Government cannot eliminate poverty or provide a bountiful economy or reduce inflation or save our cities or cure illiteracy or provide energy. And government cannot mandate goodness. Only a true partnership between government and the people can ever hope to reach these goals.

JIMMY CARTER, 39TH PRESIDENT (1977–1981)

Our whole constitutional heritage rebels at the thought of giving government the power to control men's minds.

THURGOOD MARSHALL, FORMER U.S. SUPREME COURT ASSOCIATE JUSTICE

....

Even to observe neutrality you must have a strong government.

ALEXANDER HAMILTON, U.S. STATESMAN

....

The most important issue in America these days is not tax cuts, or prescription drugs, or even improving education. The most important issue is honest government.

BILL O'REILLY, COMMENTATOR AND AUTHOR

The people of this country have their own mandate.

HOWARD ZINN, HISTORIAN AND AUTHOR

Remember that a government big enough to give you everything you want is also big enough to take away everything you have.

DAVY CROCKETT, FRONTIERSMAN AND POLITICIAN

Government exists to create and preserve conditions in which people can translate their ideas into practical reality.

GERALD R. FORD, 38TH PRESIDENT (1974–1977)

Separation of church and state cannot mean an absolute separation between moral principles and political power.

EDWARD M. KENNEDY, U.S. SENATOR

The moral test of government is how that government treats those who are in the dawn of life, the children; those who are in the twilight of life, the elderly; and those who are in the shadows of life—the sick, the needy and the handicapped.

HUBERT HUMPHREY, 38TH VICE PRESIDENT (1965–1969)

No man is good enough to govern another man without that other's consent.

ABRAHAM LINCOLN, 16TH PRESIDENT (1861–1865)

....

That government is best which governs least, because its people discipline themselves.

THOMAS JEFFERSON, 3RD PRESIDENT (1801–1809)

....

Members of the U.S. House and the U.S. Senate are not there by accident. Each managed to get there for some reason. Learn what it was and you will know something important about them, about our country and about the American people.

DONALD RUMSFELD, U.S. SECRETARY OF DEFENSE

It must be a government which submits loyally and heartily to the Constitution and the laws—the laws of the nation and the laws of the States themselves—accepting and obeying faithfully the whole Constitution as it is.

RUTHERFORD B. HAYES, 19TH PRESIDENT (1877–1881)

··

The government is in us; we are the government, you and I.

THEODORE ROOSEVELT, 26TH PRESIDENT (1901–1909)

··

We cannot permit any inquisition either within or without the law or apply any religious test to the holding of office.

CALVIN COOLIDGE, 30TH PRESIDENT (1923–1929)

Over the long haul, sustainable hope is as important to the health of self-government as sustainable development is for ecological health. Dashed hopes poison our political will just as surely as chemical waste can poison drinking water aquifers deep in the ground.

AL GORE, 45TH VICE PRESIDENT (1993–2001)

Respect for conscience is most in jeopardy, and the harmony of our diverse society is most at risk, when we re-establish, directly or indirectly, a religious test for public office.

EDWARD M. KENNEDY, U.S. SENATOR

As the happiness of the people is the sole end of government, so the consent of the people is the only foundation of it, in reason, morality, and the natural fitness of things.

JOHN ADAMS, 1ST VICE PRESIDENT (1789–1797) AND 2ND PRESIDENT (1797–1801)

The care of human life and happiness, and not their destruction, is the first and only legitimate object of good government.

THOMAS JEFFERSON, 3RD PRESIDENT (1801–1809)

The best form of government is that which is most likely to prevent the greatest sum of evil.

JAMES MONROE, 5TH PRESIDENT (1817–1825)

All great questions must be raised by great voices, and the greatest voice is the voice of the people—speaking out—in prose, or painting or poetry or music; speaking out—in homes and halls, streets and farms, courts and cafes—let that voice speak and the stillness you hear will be the gratitude of mankind.

ROBERT F. KENNEDY, FORMER ATTORNEY GENERAL AND U.S. SENATOR

....

But even the best organized government will only be as effective as the people who carry out its policies.

JIMMY CARTER, 39TH PRESIDENT (1977–1981)

No government or social system is so evil that its people must be considered as lacking in virtue.

JOHN F. KENNEDY, 35TH PRESIDENT (1961–1963)

We admit of no government by divine right. … The only legitimate right to govern is an express grant of power from the governed.

WILLIAM HENRY HARRISON, 9TH PRESIDENT (1841)

The will of the people is the only legitimate foundation of any government, and to protect its free expression should be our first object.

THOMAS JEFFERSON, 3RD PRESIDENT (1801–1809)

No foreign policy—no matter how ingenious—has any chance of success if it is born in the minds of a few and carried in the hearts of none.

HENRY KISSINGER, FOREIGN-POLICY ADVISER

....

Freedom exists only where the people take care of the government.

WOODROW WILSON, 28TH PRESIDENT (1913–1921)

....

Religious values cannot be excluded from every public issue; but not every public issue involves religious values.

EDWARD M. KENNEDY, U.S. SENATOR

We are a nation that has a government—not the other way around. And this makes us special among the nations of the earth. Our Government has no power except that granted it by the people. It is time to check and reverse the growth of government which shows signs of having grown beyond the consent of the governed.

RONALD REAGAN, 40TH PRESIDENT (1981–1989)

In framing a government which is to be administered by men over men the great difficulty lies in this: You must first enable the government to control the governed, and in the next place, oblige it to control itself.

ALEXANDER HAMILTON, U.S. STATESMAN

The citizen can bring our political and governmental institutions back to life, make them responsive and accountable, and keep them honest. No one else can.

JOHN GARDNER, NOVELIST AND POET

A nation of sheep will beget a government of wolves.

EDWARD R. MURROW, RADIO AND TELEVISION BROADCASTER

No other people have a government more worthy of their respect and love or a land so magnificent in extent, so pleasant to look upon, and so full of generous suggestion to enterprise and labor.

BENJAMIN HARRISON, 23RD PRESIDENT (1889–1893)

HOPE

—★—

Hope in the face of difficulty. Hope in the face of uncertainty. The audacity of hope! In the end, that is God's greatest gift to us, the bedrock of this nation. A belief in things not seen. A belief that there are better days ahead.

OBAMA BARACK, U.S. SENATOR

Most of the important things in the world have been accomplished by people who have kept on trying when there seemed to be no hope at all.

DALE CARNEGIE, AUTHOR AND PUBLIC SPEAKER

This great, rich, restless country can offer opportunity and education and hope to all; black and white, North and South, sharecropper or city dweller.

LYNDON B. JOHNSON, 36TH PRESIDENT (1963–1969)

The mystic chords of memory … will yet swell the chorus of the Union, when again touched, as surely they will be, by the better angels of our nature.

ABRAHAM LINCOLN, 16TH PRESIDENT (1861–1865)

Failure is not an American habit, and in the strength of great hope we must all shoulder our common load.

FRANKLIN DELANO ROOSEVELT, 32ND PRESIDENT (1933–1945)

As a nation, our greatest export has always been hope: hope that through the rule of law people can be free to pursue their dreams, that democracy can supplant repression and that justice, not power, will be the guiding force in society. Our moral authority in the world derived from the hope anchored in the rule of law.

AL GORE, 45TH VICE PRESIDENT (1993–2001)

The poet's voice need not merely be the record of man, it can be one of the props, the pillars to help him endure and prevail.

WILLIAM FAULKNER, NOBEL PRIZE-WINNING AUTHOR

....

Optimism is a force multiplier.

COLIN POWELL, FORMER SECRETARY OF STATE

....

Our problems are man-made—therefore, they can be solved by man. And man can be as big as he wants.

JOHN F. KENNEDY, 35TH PRESIDENT (1961–1963)

We have confidence because freedom is the permanent hope of mankind, the hunger in dark places, the longing of the soul.

GEORGE W. BUSH, 43RD PRESIDENT (2001–   )

When hope is taken away from a people moral, degeneration follows swiftly after.

PEARL S. BUCK, NOBEL PRIZE-WINNING AUTHOR

We have to have faith that even when the majority seems to decide as we think wrongly, we still believe the fundamental principles that we have laid down, and we wait for the day to come when the thing that we believe is right becomes the majority decision of the people.

ELEANOR ROOSEVELT, FORMER FIRST LADY AND UNITED NATIONS DELEGATE

With the leadership of this President and the resilient spirit of the American people, we will meet the challenges of our time and carry the gift of freedom forward to the future.

DICK CHENEY, 46TH VICE PRESIDENT (2001–   )

Our hopes must be tempered with the caution of history—but with our hopes go the hopes of all mankind.

JOHN F. KENNEDY, 35TH PRESIDENT (1961–1963)

Our beliefs in religious freedom, political freedom, and economic freedom—that's what makes an American. Our belief in democracy, the rule of law, and respect for human life—that's how you become an American. It is these very principles—and the opportunities these principles give to so many to create a better life for themselves and their families—that make America, and New York, a "shining city on a hill."

RUDOLPH GIULIANI, FORMER MAYOR OF NEW YORK CITY

The world you inherit today may not always be an easy one, for nothing worth winning is easily gained.

RONALD REAGAN, 40TH PRESIDENT (1981–1989)

My country owes me nothing. It gave me, as it gives every boy and girl, a chance. It gave me schooling, independence of action, opportunity for service and honor. In no other land could a boy from a country village, without inheritance or influential friends, look forward with unbounded hope.

HERBERT HOOVER, 31ST PRESIDENT (1929–1933)

History, despite its wrenching pain, cannot be unlived, but if faced with courage, need not be lived again.

MAYA ANGELOU, POET AND WRITER

This, then, is the state of the union: free and restless, growing and full of hope. So it was in the beginning. So it shall always be, while God is willing, and we are strong enough to keep the faith.

LYNDON B. JOHNSON, 36TH PRESIDENT (1963–1969)

This great nation will endure as it has endured, will revive and will prosper.

FRANKLIN DELANO ROOSEVELT, 32ND PRESIDENT (1933–1945)

If you lose hope, somehow you lose the vitality that keeps life moving, you lose that courage to be, that quality that helps you go on in spite of it all. And so today I still have a dream.

MARTIN LUTHER KING, JR., CIVIL RIGHTS LEADER

Some people see things as they are and say, "Why?" I dream things that never were and say, "Why not?"

ROBERT F. KENNEDY, FORMER ATTORNEY GENERAL

....

But we believed if we kept on working, if we kept on marching, if we kept on voting, if we kept on believing, we would make America beautiful for everybody.

AL SHARPTON, FOUNDER OF THE NATIONAL YOUTH MOVEMENT

Today I can declare my hope and declare it from the bottom of my heart that we will eventually see the time when that number of nuclear weapons is down to zero and the world is a much better place.

COLIN POWELL, FORMER SECRETARY OF STATE

We simply must have faith in each other, faith in our ability to govern ourselves, and faith in the future of this Nation.

JIMMY CARTER, 39TH PRESIDENT (1977–1981)

Clouds and darkness surround us, yet Heaven is just, and the day of triumph will surely come, when justice and truth will be vindicated. Our wrongs will be made right, and we will once more, taste the blessings of freedom.

MARY TODD LINCOLN, FORMER FIRST LADY

For other nations, utopia is a blessed past never to be recovered; for Americans it is just beyond the horizon.

HENRY KISSINGER, FOREIGN-POLICY ADVISER

We here in America, hold in our hands the hope of the world, the fate of the coming years; and shame and disgrace will be ours if, in our eyes, the light of high resolve is dimmed, if we trail in the dust the golden hopes of men.

THEODORE ROOSEVELT, 26TH PRESIDENT (1901–1909)

I steer my bark with hope in the head, leaving fear astern. My hopes indeed sometimes fail, but not oftener than the forebodings of the gloomy.

THOMAS JEFFERSON, 3RD PRESIDENT (1801–1809)

It is the nature of man to rise to greatness if greatness is expected of him.

JOHN STEINBECK, NOBEL PRIZE-WINNING AUTHOR

IDEALS

—★—

Let us dedicate ourselves to what the Greeks wrote so many years ago: to tame the savageness of man and make gentle the life of this world.

ROBERT F. KENNEDY, FORMER ATTORNEY GENERAL AND U.S. SENATOR

Be courageous. I have seen many depressions in business. Always America has emerged from these stronger and more prosperous. Be brave as your fathers before you. Have faith! Go forward!

THOMAS EDISON, INVENTOR

It's important to believe in yourself and when you feel like you have the right idea, to stay with it.

ROSA PARKS, CIVIL RIGHTS PIONEER

Because America is now closer to its ideals, your birthright, your inheritance is a freer, more just, strong, confident and wealthy nation in which you can make your way according to your talents and your dreams.

CONDOLEEZZA RICE, SECRETARY OF STATE AND FORMER NATIONAL SECURITY ADVISOR

Idealism is needed in American.

GEORGE W. BUSH, 43RD PRESIDENT (2001–)

When will our conscience grow so tender that we will act to prevent human misery rather than avenge it?

ELEANOR ROOSEVELT, FORMER FIRST LADY AND UNITED NATIONS DELEGATE

I hold the maxim no less applicable to public than to private affairs that honesty is always the best policy.

GEORGE WASHINGTON, 1ST PRESIDENT (1789–1797)

If you do the things you think you cannot do, you'll feel your resistance, your hope, your dignity, and your courage grow stronger every time you prove it.

JOHN MCCAIN, U.S. SENATOR

....

A man may die, nations may rise and fall, but an idea lives on.

JOHN F. KENNEDY, 35TH PRESIDENT (1961–1963)

....

Whatever you want in life, other people are going to want it too. Believe in yourself enough to accept the idea that you have an equal right to it.

DIANE SAWYER, NEWS ANCHOR AND REPORTER

Our mission is at once the oldest and the most basic of this country: to right wrong, to do justice, to serve man.

LYNDON B. JOHNSON, 36TH PRESIDENT (1963–1969)

Our country, like any, is composed of humans and therefore is flawed. We are not always right in our actions and judgments, but I know from the experience of my own life the importance and rightness of America's ideals.

MADELEINE ALBRIGHT, FORMER SECRETARY OF STATE

....

Ideas control the world.

JAMES GARFIELD, 20TH PRESIDENT (1881)

....

We must adjust to changing times and still hold to unchanging principles.

JIMMY CARTER, 39TH PRESIDENT (1977–1981)

Our heritage and ideals, our code and standards—the things we live by and teach our children—are preserved or diminished by how freely we exchange ideas and feelings.

WALT DISNEY, ANIMATOR AND ENTERTAINMENT EXECUTIVE

An idealist is a person who helps other people to be prosperous.

HENRY FORD, INDUSTRIALIST AND AUTOMOBILE MANUFACTURER

Cynics will say we have lost our way, that the American century is at its end. But the cynics are wrong. America is still the model to which the world aspires. Almost everywhere in the world the values that the United States has proclaimed, defended, and tried to live are now rising.

AL GORE, 45TH VICE PRESIDENT (1993–2001)

A good society is able to face schemes of world domination and foreign revolutions alike without fear.

FRANKLIN DELANO ROOSEVELT, 32ND PRESIDENT (1933–1945)

The foundation of American society rests on a set of enduring, defining values: Faith in God, the sanctity of human life, the existence of right and wrong, and the certain knowledge that we're all ultimately accountable for our actions.

TOM DELAY, MAJORITY LEADER OF THE U.S. HOUSE OF REPRESENTATIVES

The "morality of compromise" sounds contradictory. Compromise is usually a sign of weakness, or an admission of defeat. Strong men don't compromise, it is said, and principles should never be compromised.

ANDREW CARNEGIE, INDUSTRIALIST AND PHILANTHROPIST

There is no force so democratic as the force of an ideal.

CALVIN COOLIDGE, 30TH PRESIDENT (1923–1929)

Ideals are like stars: You will not succeed in touching them with your hands, but like the seafaring man on the desert of waters, you choose them as your guides, and following them you reach your destiny.

CARL SCHURZ, POLITICIAN AND JOURNALIST

We do not see faith, hope and charity as unattainable ideals, but we use them as stout supports of a Nation fighting the fight for freedom in a modern civilization.

FRANKLIN DELANO ROOSEVELT, 32ND PRESIDENT (1933–1945)

There is no substitute for hard work.

THOMAS EDISON, INVENTOR

The greatest responsibility of a society is the transmission of values—values of freedom, equality, and justice—from one generation to the next.

JOHN ASHCROFT, FORMER U.S. ATTORNEY GENERAL

We must always remember that while America cherishes the ideals of equality, justice, and the rule of law, we do not own them.

CONDOLEEZZA RICE, SECRETARY OF STATE AND FORMER NATIONAL SECURITY ADVISOR

....

If humanity does not opt for integrity, we are through completely. It is absolutely touch and go. Each one of us could make the difference.

R. BUCKMINSTER FULLER, ARCHITECT AND ENGINEER

A people that values its privileges above its principles soon loses both.

Dwight D. Eisenhower, 34th President (1953–1961)

···

You've got to be tough about what you believe in, and then, when people need help,
you've got to be willing to help them.

Rudolph Giuliani, Former Mayor of New York City

···

This nation will not be better off because we have one more millionaire, but
will be better if one more person lives his or her life with integrity serving
his or her fellow man.

Jerry Moran, U.S. Representative

What we need in the world is manners. … I think that if, instead of preach-
ing brotherly love, we preached good manners, we might get a little further.
It sounds less righteous and more practical.

Eleanor Roosevelt, Former First Lady and United Nations Delegate

All of us have a chance to be made great—not by our achievements, measured
in the world's eyes—but through our commitment to a path of righteousness,
and to one another.

Al Gore, 45th Vice President (1993–2001)

The ideals which have lighted my way, and time after time have given me new courage to face life cheerfully have been kindness, beauty, and truth.

ALBERT EINSTEIN, NOBEL PRIZE-WINNING PHYSICIST

Ideals are an imaginative understanding of that which is desirable in that which is possible.

WALTER LIPPMANN, PULITZER PRIZE-WINNING COLUMNIST

It is not a field of a few acres of ground, but a cause, that we are defending, and whether we defeat the enemy in one battle, or by degrees, the consequences will be the same.

THOMAS PAINE, AMERICAN REVOLUTIONARY

With the idealism and fair play which are the core of our system and our strength, we can have a strong and prosperous America at peace with itself and the world.

RONALD REAGAN, 40TH PRESIDENT (1981–1989)

Honesty is the first chapter in the book of wisdom.

THOMAS JEFFERSON, 3RD PRESIDENT (1801–1809)

An ideal cannot wait for its realization to prove its validity.

GEORGE SANTAYANA, PHILOSOPHER, POET, AND HUMANIST

If you have built castles in the air your work need not be lost; that is where they should be. Now put foundations under them.

HENRY DAVID THOREAU, ESSAYIST

Parents are usually more careful to bestow knowledge on their children rather than virtue, the art of speaking well rather than doing well; but their manners should be of the greatest concern.

R. BUCKMINSTER FULLER, ARCHITECT AND ENGINEER

Let's have faith that right makes might; and in that faith let us, to the end, dare to do our duty as we understand it.

ABRAHAM LINCOLN, 16TH PRESIDENT (1861–1865)

The truth is America's most potent weapon. We cannot enlarge upon the truth. But we can and must intensify our efforts to make that truth more shining.

RICHARD M. NIXON, 37TH PRESIDENT (1969–1974)

I was raised to believe that excellence is the best deterrent to racism or sexism. And that's how I operate my life.

OPRAH WINFREY, TELEVISION TALK-SHOW HOST, ACTRESS, AND PRODUCER

Peace is normally a great good, and normally it coincides with righteousness, but it is righteousness and not peace which should bind the conscience of a nation as it should bind the conscience of an individual; and neither a nation nor an individual can surrender conscience to another's keeping.

THEODORE ROOSEVELT, 26TH PRESIDENT (1901–1909)

One who condones evils is just as guilty as the one who perpetrates it.

MARTIN LUTHER KING, JR., CIVIL RIGHTS LEADER

To make the public sentiment, on the side of all that is just and true and noble, is the highest use of life.

LUCY STONE, WOMEN'S SUFFRAGE LEADER

Our differences are policies, our agreements principles.

WILLIAM MCKINLEY, 25TH PRESIDENT (1897–1901)

Young America, dream. Choose the human race over the nuclear race. Bury the weapons and don't burn the people. Dream—dream of a new value system.

JESSE JACKSON, CIVIL RIGHTS LEADER

Right is more precious than peace.

WOODROW WILSON, 28TH PRESIDENT (1913–1921)

We are not afraid to follow truth wherever it may lead, nor to tolerate any error so long as reason is left free to combat it.

THOMAS JEFFERSON, 3RD PRESIDENT (1801–1809)

The truly important ingredients of life are still the same as they always have been—true love and real friendship, honesty and faithfulness, sincerity, unselfishness and selflessness, the concept that it is better to give than to receive, to do unto others as you would have them do unto you. These principles are still around, they haven't gone away.

NANCY REAGAN, FORMER FIRST LADY

An absence of complacency should not provoke an absence of confidence.

JOHN MCCAIN, U.S. SENATOR

My country is the world, and my religion is to do good.

THOMAS PAINE, AMERICAN REVOLUTIONARY

Great minds discuss ideas, mediocre minds discuss events, small minds discuss personalities.

ELEANOR ROOSEVELT, FORMER FIRST LADY AND UNITED NATIONS DELEGATE

INGENUITY

★

You can never solve a problem on the level on which it was created.
ALBERT EINSTEIN, NOBEL PRIZE-WINNING PHYSICIST

Americans have always reached for the impossible, looked to the next horizon, and asked: What if?
JOHN KERRY, U.S. SENATOR

Never tell people how to do things. Tell them what to do and they will surprise you with their ingenuity.
GENERAL GEORGE S. PATTON

Towering genius disdains a beaten path. It seeks regions hitherto unexplored.
ABRAHAM LINCOLN, 16TH PRESIDENT (1861–1865)

Life is a great adventure. A series of journeys within journeys, circles within circles. And like all great journeys, they begin with a dream.
ROBERT BALLARD, EXPLORER

Discovery is the ability to be puzzled by simple things.
NOAM CHOMSKY, LINGUIST AND POLITICAL ACTIVIST

Happiness lies not in the mere possession of money, it lies in the joy of achievement, in the thrill of creative effort.

FRANKLIN DELANO ROOSEVELT, 32ND PRESIDENT (1933–1945)

Every great advance in science has issued from a new audacity of the imagination.

JOHN DEWEY, PHILOSOPHER AND EDUCATION

Being true to yourself really means being true to all the complexities of the human spirit.

RITA DOVE, FORMER U.S. POET LAUREATE

....

Together let us explore the stars, conquer the deserts, eradicate disease, tap the ocean depths and encourage the arts and commerce.

JOHN F. KENNEDY, 35TH PRESIDENT (1961–1963)

....

The one thing that we, in the United States today, still do better than any other country in the world, is to build a better mousetrap.

ADMIRAL ALAN SHEPARD, JR., ASTRONAUT

In an epic journey, after you have a dream, you begin to prepare yourself to pursue that dream.

ROBERT BALLARD, EXPLORER

Man's reason and spirit have often solved the seemingly unsolvable—and we believe they can do it again.

JOHN F. KENNEDY, 35TH PRESIDENT (1961–1963)

Nothing in this world can take the place of persistence. Talent will not; nothing is more common than unsuccessful people with talent. Genius will not; unrewarded genius is almost a proverb. Education will not; the world is full of educated derelicts. Persistence and determination alone are omnipotent. The slogan "press on" has solved and always will solve the problems of the human race.

CALVIN COOLIDGE, 30TH PRESIDENT (1923–1929)

Without imagination, we can go nowhere.

RITA DOVE, FORMER U.S. POET LAUREATE

INTERNATIONAL RELATIONS

The first requisite of peace among nations is common adherence to the principle that governments derive their just powers from the consent of the governed.

HARRY S. TRUMAN, 33RD PRESIDENT (1945–1953)

The nation which indulges toward another an habitual hatred or an habitual fondness is in some degree a slave.

GEORGE WASHINGTON, 1ST PRESIDENT (1789–1797)

We believe that reform will ultimately be successful because freedom and democracy are powerful universal values, not just Western or American values.

COLIN POWELL, FORMER SECRETARY OF STATE

For good or ill, we live in an interdependent world. We can't escape each other.

WILLIAM J. CLINTON, 42ND PRESIDENT (1993–2001)

Let historians not record that when America was the most powerful nation in the world we passed on the other side of the road and allowed the last hopes for peace and freedom of millions of people to be suffocated by the forces of totalitarianism.

RICHARD M. NIXON, 37TH PRESIDENT (1969–1974)

Genuine peace must be the product of many nations, the sum of many acts. It must be dynamic, not static, changing to meet the challenge of each new generation. For peace is a process—a way of solving problems.

JOHN F. KENNEDY, 35TH PRESIDENT (1961–1963)

We can no longer separate the traditional issues of war and peace from the new global questions of justice, equity, and human rights.

JIMMY CARTER, 39TH PRESIDENT (1977–1981)

I do not believe we should be too quick to criticize the actions of a belligerent nation. There is always the question whether we, ourselves, would do better under similar circumstances.

CHARLES LINDBERGH, AVIATOR AND PULITZER PRIZE-WINNING AUTHOR

The world must learn to work together, or finally it will not work at all.

DWIGHT D. EISENHOWER, 34TH PRESIDENT (1953–1961)

....

America is blessed to be a land that is touched by every other land, and in turn we touch every other land.

COLIN POWELL, FORMER SECRETARY OF STATE

I find it, unhappily, necessary to report that the future and the safety of our country and of our democracy are overwhelmingly involved in events far beyond our borders.

FRANKLIN DELANO ROOSEVELT, 32ND PRESIDENT (1933–1945)

The free peoples of the world look to us for support in maintaining their freedom.

HARRY S. TRUMAN, 33RD PRESIDENT (1945–1953)

Taking care always to keep ourselves by suitable establishments on a respectable defensive posture, we may safely trust to temporary alliances for extraordinary emergencies.

GEORGE WASHINGTON, 1ST PRESIDENT (1789–1797)

Anyone who feels that we can live without being concerned about other individuals and other nations is sleeping through a revolution.

MARTIN LUTHER KING, JR., CIVIL RIGHTS LEADER

Every nation that benefits from living on the right side of the freedom divide has an obligation to share freedom's blessings.

CONDOLEEZZA RICE, SECRETARY OF STATE AND FORMER NATIONAL SECURITY ADVISOR

Our aim is to build and preserve a community of free and independent nations, with governments that answer to their citizens, and reflect their own cultures. And because democracies respect their own people and their neighbors, the advance of freedom will lead to peace.

GEORGE W. BUSH, 43RD PRESIDENT (2001–   )

We know a peaceful world cannot long exist one-third rich and two-thirds hungry.

JIMMY CARTER, 39TH PRESIDENT (1977–1981)

We are but one of the champions of the rights of mankind.

WOODROW WILSON, 28TH PRESIDENT (1913–1921)

I believe that it must be the policy of the United States to support free peoples who are resisting attempted subjugation by armed minorities or by outside pressure.

HARRY S. TRUMAN, 33RD PRESIDENT (1945–1953)

....

Antipathy in one nation against another disposes each more readily to offer insult and injury.

GEORGE WASHINGTON, 1ST PRESIDENT (1789–1797)

America's formidable power must continue to be deployed on behalf of principles that are simultaneously American, but that are also beyond and greater than ourselves.

COLIN POWELL, FORMER SECRETARY OF STATE

World peace, like community peace, does not require that each man love his neighbor—it requires only that they live together in mutual tolerance, submitting their disputes to a just and peaceful settlement.

JOHN F. KENNEDY, 35TH PRESIDENT (1961–1963)

We realize that America's leadership and prestige depend, not merely upon our unmatched material progress, riches and military strength, but on how we use our power in the interests of world peace and human betterment.

DWIGHT D. EISENHOWER, 34TH PRESIDENT (1953–1961)

God grant that not only the love of liberty but a thorough knowledge of the rights of man may pervade all the nations of the earth, so that a philosopher may set his foot anywhere on its surface and say: This is my country!

BENJAMIN FRANKLIN, STATESMAN AND SCIENTIST

JUSTICE

— ⭐ —

Equal and exact justice to all men, of whatever state or persuasion, religious or political, peace, commerce, and host friendship with all nations, entangling alliances with none.

THOMAS JEFFERSON, 3RD PRESIDENT (1801–1809)

Our finest moments have come when we have faithfully served the cause of justice for our own citizens, and for the people of other lands. And through our nation's history, we have turned to prayer for wisdom to know the good, and for the courage to do the good.

GEORGE W. BUSH, 43RD PRESIDENT (2001–)

Justice has nothing to do with expediency. Justice has nothing to do with any temporary standard whatever. It is rooted and grounded in the fundamental instincts of humanity.

WOODROW WILSON, 28TH PRESIDENT (1913–1921)

It is of great importance in a republic not only to guard against the oppression of its rulers, but to guard one part of society against the injustice of the other part.

ALEXANDER HAMILTON, U.S. STATESMAN

The biggest corporation, like the humblest private citizen, must be held to strict compliance with the will of the people.

THEODORE ROOSEVELT, 26TH PRESIDENT (1901–1909)

Compassion is no substitute for justice.

RUSH LIMBAUGH, AUTHOR AND COMMENTATOR

When a just cause reaches its flood tide ... whatever stands in the way must fall before its overwhelming power.

CARRIE CHAPMAN CATT, WOMEN'S SUFFRAGE LEADER

....

Injustice anywhere is a threat to justice everywhere.

MARTIN LUTHER KING, JR., CIVIL RIGHTS LEADER

....

Justice is the end of government. It is the end of civil society. It ever has been and ever will be pursued until it be obtained, or until liberty be lost in the pursuit.

JAMES MADISON, 4TH PRESIDENT (1809–1817)

We must remember that any oppression, any injustice, any hatred, is a wedge designed to attack our civilization.

FRANKLIN DELANO ROOSEVELT, 32ND PRESIDENT (1933–1945)

Whether we bring our enemies to justice, or bring justice to our enemies, justice will be done.

GEORGE W. BUSH, 43RD PRESIDENT (2001–)

....

Justice cannot be for one side alone, but must be for both.

ELEANOR ROOSEVELT, FORMER FIRST LADY

....

It is the responsibility of all citizens in all sections of this country to respect the rights of all others and to respect the law of the land.

JOHN F. KENNEDY, 35TH PRESIDENT (1961–1963)

Power at its best is love implementing the demands of justice. Justice at its best is love correcting everything that stands against love.

MARTIN LUTHER KING, JR., CIVIL RIGHTS LEADER

Justice remains the greatest power on earth. To that tremendous power alone will we submit.

HARRY S. TRUMAN, 33RD PRESIDENT (1945–1953)

Justice, sir, is the great interest of man on earth. It is the ligament which holds civilized beings and civilized nations together.

DANIEL WEBSTER, STATESMAN AND LAWYER

The administration of justice is the firmest pillar of government.
GEORGE WASHINGTON, 1ST PRESIDENT (1789–1797)

A society that has more justice is a society that needs less charity.
RALPH NADER, THIRD-PARTY PRESIDENTIAL NOMINEE

In order to form a more perfect union, our Founding Fathers set forth a system of justice in which Americans are not passive spectators but active participants; a system that honors equally the rights of all Americans by making justice available and accessible to all.
JOHN ASHCROFT, FORMER U.S. ATTORNEY GENERAL

....

Judging from the main portions of the history of the world, so far, justice is always in jeopardy.

WALT WHITMAN, POET AND ESSAYIST

....

I'm for truth, no matter who tells it. I'm for justice, no matter who it's for or against.
MALCOLM X, MUSLIM LEADER

LEADERSHIP

— ★ —

American leadership has been a mighty force for human progress. The steady march of democracy and free enterprise across the globe speaks to the steadfastness of our leadership and the power of our ideals.

OBAMA BARACK, U.S. SENATOR

A team means up, down and sideways. I'm a great believer in loyalty to the person I work for. If you take the King's shilling, you do the King's work. And so, loyalty upward is a very important trait for me. Loyalty downward, to those who are doing it for you. And loyalty to the people you're working side by side with.

COLIN POWELL, FORMER SECRETARY OF STATE

In choosing a president, we really don't choose a Republican or Democrat, a conservative or liberal. We choose a leader.

RUDOLPH GIULIANI, FORMER MAYOR OF NEW YORK CITY

The way I work is to identify the problem, find the right individuals to do the job, and then let them go to it. I've found this invariably brings out the best in people.

RONALD REAGAN, 40TH PRESIDENT (1981–1989)

Leadership has a harder job to do than just choose sides. It must bring sides together.

JESSE JACKSON, CIVIL RIGHTS LEADER

Moments come along in history when leaders must make fundamental decisions about how to confront a long term challenge abroad and how best to keep the American people secure.

DICK CHENEY, 46TH VICE PRESIDENT (2001–)

If your actions inspire others to dream more, learn more, do more and become more, you are a leader.

JOHN QUINCY ADAMS, 6TH PRESIDENT (1825–1829)

Leadership is a potent combination of strategy and character. But if you must be without one, be without the strategy.

GENERAL H. NORMAN SCHWARZKOPF

....

You will never make a good leader unless you have learned to follow.

ROBERT BALLARD, EXPLORER

....

The function of leadership is to produce more leaders, not more followers.

RALPH NADER, THIRD-PARTY PRESIDENTIAL NOMINEE

In every dark hour of our national life a leadership of frankness and vigor has met with that understanding and support of the people themselves which is essential to victory.

FRANKLIN DELANO ROOSEVELT, 32ND PRESIDENT (1933–1945)

Leadership is all about people. It is not about organizations. It is not about plans. It is not about strategies. It is all about people—motivating people to get the job done. You have to be people-centered.

COLIN POWELL, FORMER SECRETARY OF STATE

When you give someone a responsibility and authority, they don't mind being accountable.

DANIEL S. GOLDIN, FORMER NASA ADMINISTRATOR

The gap between our citizens and our Government has never been so wide. The people are looking for honest answers, not easy answers; clear leadership, not false claims and evasiveness and politics as usual.

JIMMY CARTER, 39TH PRESIDENT (1977–1981)

Blessed are the people whose leaders can look destiny in the eye without flinching but also without attempting to play God.

HENRY KISSINGER, FOREIGN-POLICY ADVISER

Outstanding leaders go out of the way to boost the self-esteem of their personnel. If people believe in themselves, it's amazing what they can accomplish.

SAM WALTON, FOUNDER OF WAL-MART STORES, INC.

The true test of character comes when the stakes are high, when the chips are down, when your gut starts to turn, when the sweat starts to form on your brow, when you know the decision you are about to make may not be popular, but it *must* be made.

GENERAL CHARLES C. KRULAK

....

We herd sheep, we drive cattle, we lead people. Lead me, follow me, or get out of my way.

GENERAL GEORGE S. PATTON

....

You have to enable and empower people to make decisions independent of you. As I've learned, each person on a team is an extension of your leadership; if they feel empowered by you they will magnify your power to lead. Trust is a great force multiplier.

TOM RIDGE, FORMER HOMELAND SECURITY ADVISOR

Leadership rests not only upon ability, not only upon capacity; having the capacity to lead is not enough. The leader must be willing to use it. His leadership is then based on truth and character. There must be truth in the purpose and willpower in the character.

VINCE LOMBARDI, FORMER FOOTBALL COACH

It is precisely because I have experienced so much of our past, that I have no fears for our future. Not so long as this institution continues to attract men and women who are patriots as well as partisans—legislators who combine idealism and realism, and who answer to posterity rather than polltakers. For anyone can take a poll. Only a true leader can move a nation.

BOB DOLE, FORMER U.S. SENATE MAJORITY LEADER

Don't speak ill of your predecessors or successors. You didn't walk in their shoes.

DONALD RUMSFELD, U.S. SECRETARY OF DEFENSE

The task of the leader is to get his people from where they are to where they have not been.

HENRY KISSINGER, FOREIGN-POLICY ADVISER

Failures proclaim lost leadership, obscure purpose, weakening wills and the risk of inciting our sworn enemies to new aggressions and to new excesses.

BARRY GOLDWATER, FORMER U.S. SENATOR

Trust is the essence of leadership.

COLIN POWELL, FORMER SECRETARY OF STATE

The best leader is the one who has sense enough to pick good men to do what he wants done, and self-restraint enough to keep from meddling with them while they do it.

THEODORE ROOSEVELT, 26TH PRESIDENT (1901–1909)

Leadership is not managing an organization. Organizations are made up of people. Leadership is motivating people. Leadership is about people.

GENERAL H. NORMAN SCHWARZKOPF

Men make history and not the other way around. In periods where there is no leadership, society stands still. Progress occurs when courageous, skillful leaders seize the opportunity to change things for the better.

HARRY S. TRUMAN, 33RD PRESIDENT (1945–1953)

This, then, is the test we must set for ourselves; not to march alone but to march in such a way that others will wish to join us.

HUBERT HUMPHREY, 38TH VICE PRESIDENT (1965–1969)

....

Produce great men, the rest follows.

WALT WHITMAN, POET AND ESSAYIST

....

Great nations are simply the operating fronts of behind-the-scenes, vastly ambitious individuals who had become so effectively powerful because of their ability to remain invisible while operating behind the national scenery.

R. BUCKMINSTER FULLER, ARCHITECT AND ENGINEER

PATRIOTISM

──────── ★ ────────

We have every right to dream heroic dreams. Those who say that we're in a time when there are not heroes, they just don't know where to look.

RONALD REAGAN, 40TH PRESIDENT (1981–1989)

Look upon this picture of happiness and honor and say, "We too are citizens of America."

ANDREW JACKSON, 7TH PRESIDENT (1829–1837)

Four score and seven years ago our fathers brought forth on this continent, a new nation, conceived in Liberty, and dedicated to the proposition that all men are created equal.

ABRAHAM LINCOLN, 16TH PRESIDENT (1861–1865)

Today, we're all red, white, and blue.

WILLIAM J. CLINTON, 42ND PRESIDENT (1993–2001)

We see in our country today the evidence of a core value that, in my view, was dormant for a time: patriotism, a core value; constant, deep patriotism by those who salute the flag and by those who wave the flag.

GENERAL TOMMY FRANKS

What do we mean by patriotism in the context of our times? I venture to suggest that what we mean is a sense of national responsibility ... a patriotism which is not short, frenzied outbursts of emotion, but the tranquil and steady dedication of a lifetime.

ADLAI STEVENSON, FORMER GOVERNOR OF ILLINOIS AND DIPLOMAT

Better than any law or rule or threat of punishment would be the moving strength of our own good example, demonstrating our lack of hypocrisy, proving the beauty and worth of our instruction.

MARIO CUOMO, FORMER GOVERNOR OF NEW YORK

With a good conscience our only sure reward, with history the final judge of our deeds, let us go forth to lead the land we love.

JOHN F. KENNEDY, 35TH PRESIDENT (1961–1963)

We are Americans first, Americans last, Americans always.

JOHN MCCAIN, U.S. SENATOR

I shall know but one country. The ends I aim at shall be my country's, my God's and Truth's. I was born an American; I live an American; I shall die an American.

DANIEL WEBSTER, STATESMAN AND LAWYER

Patriotism is easy to understand in America; it means looking out for your-self by looking out for your country.

CALVIN COOLIDGE, 30TH PRESIDENT (1923–1929)

···

I only regret that I have but one life to lose for my country.

NATHAN HALE, AMERICAN REVOLUTIONARY LEADER

···

To me, being a citizen of the United States of America is the greatest honor and privilege in this world.

GERALD R. FORD, 38TH PRESIDENT (1974–1977)

But with all the imperfections of our present government, it is without com-parison the best existing, or that ever did exist.

THOMAS JEFFERSON, 3RD PRESIDENT (1801–1809)

Intellectually I know that America is no better than any other country; emotionally I know she is better than every other country.

SINCLAIR LEWIS, NOBEL PRIZE-WINNING AUTHOR

It was Washington's influence that made Lincoln and all other real patriots the Republic has known. …

MARK TWAIN, AUTHOR AND HUMORIST

There can be no fifty-fifty Americanism in this country. There is room here for only 100% Americanism, only for those who are Americans and nothing else.

THEODORE ROOSEVELT, 26TH PRESIDENT (1901–1909)

One loves American above all things, for her youth, her greenness, her plasticity, innocence, good intentions, friends, everything.

WILLIAM JENNINGS BRYAN, STATESMAN

A dam built across a great river is impressive. ... A rich harvest in a hungry land is impressive. The sight of healthy children in a classroom is impressive. These—not mighty arms—are the achievements which the American Nation believes to be impressive.

LYNDON B. JOHNSON, 36TH PRESIDENT (1963–1969)

Since this country was founded, each generation of Americans has been summoned to give testimony to its national loyalty.

JOHN F. KENNEDY, 35TH PRESIDENT (1961–1963)

....

No country is more loved by its people.

HERBERT HOOVER, 31ST PRESIDENT (1929–1933)

....

Once you begin a great movement, there's no telling where it will end. We meant to change a nation, and instead, we changed a world.

RONALD REAGAN, 40TH PRESIDENT (1981–1989)

Patriotism is proven in our concern for others—a willingness to sacrifice for people we may never have met or seen.

GEORGE W. BUSH, 43RD PRESIDENT (2001–)

....

Our country, right or wrong. When right, to be kept right; when wrong, to be put right.

CARL SCHURZ, POLITICIAN AND JOURNALIST

....

May we be ever unswerving in devotion to principle, confident but humble with power, diligent in pursuit of the Nation's great goals.

DWIGHT D. EISENHOWER, 34TH PRESIDENT (1953–1961)

And may that Being who is supreme over all, the Patron of Order, the Fountain of Justice, and the Protector in all ages of the world of virtuous liberty, continue His blessing upon this nation and its Government and give it all possible success and duration consistent with the ends of His providence.

JOHN ADAMS, 1ST VICE PRESIDENT (1789–1797) AND 2ND PRESIDENT (1797–1801)

As a nation, we may take pride in the fact that we are soft-hearted; but we cannot afford to be soft-headed.

FRANKLIN DELANO ROOSEVELT, 32ND PRESIDENT (1933–1945)

Each man must for himself alone decide what is right and what is wrong, which course is patriotic and which isn't. You cannot shirk this and be a man. To decide against your conviction is to be an unqualified and excusable traitor, both to yourself and to your country, let me label you as they may.

MARK TWAIN, AUTHOR AND HUMORIST

An informed patriotism is what we want. And are we doing a good enough job teaching our children what America is and what she represents in the long history of the world?

RONALD REAGAN, 40TH PRESIDENT (1981–1989)

Let the word go forth from this time and place, to friend and foe alike, that the torch has been passed to a new generation of Americans—born in this century, tempered by war, disciplined by a hard and bitter peace.

JOHN F. KENNEDY, 35TH PRESIDENT (1961–1963)

....

Whenever you have a chance, say something good about our country.

JIMMY CARTER, 39TH PRESIDENT (1977–1981)

....

Our greatness as a nation has been our capacity to do what had to be done when we knew our course was right.

RICHARD M. NIXON, 37TH PRESIDENT (1969–1974)

The real test of patriotism is how we treat the men and women who put their lives on the line every day to defend our values.

JOHN EDWARDS, FORMER U.S. SENATOR

....

Patriotism is our obligation to those who have gone before us, to those who will follow us, and to those who have died for us.

GEORGE W. BUSH, 43RD PRESIDENT (2001–)

....

I always consider the settlement of America with reverence and wonder, as the opening of a grand scene and design in providence, for the illumination of the ignorant and the emancipation of the slavish part of mankind all over the earth.

JOHN ADAMS, 1ST VICE PRESIDENT (1789–1797) AND 2ND PRESIDENT (1797–1801)

I wasn't a great communicator, but I communicated great things, and they didn't spring full bloom from my brow, they came from the heart of a great nation—from our experience, our wisdom, and our belief in the principles that have guided us for two centuries.

RONALD REAGAN, 40TH PRESIDENT (1981–1989)

There are those things that at one time we all accepted as more important than our comfort or discomfort, if not our very lives. Duty, honor, country! There was a time when all was to be set aside for these. The plow was left idle, the hearth without fire, the homestead, abandoned.

CLARENCE THOMAS, U.S. SUPREME COURT ASSOCIATE JUSTICE

For this is what America is all about. It is the uncrossed desert and the unclimbed ridge. It is the star that is not reached and the harvest that is sleeping in the unplowed ground.

LYNDON B. JOHNSON, 36TH PRESIDENT (1963–1969)

No matter the nationality, no matter the religion, no matter the ethnic background, America brings out the best in people.

ARNOLD SCHWARZENEGGER, GOVERNOR OF CALIFORNIA

Behold a republic standing erect while empires all around are bowed beneath the weight of their own armaments—a republic whose flag is loved while other flags are only feared.

WILLIAM JENNINGS BRYAN, STATESMAN

It is a common observation here that our cause is the cause of all mankind, and that we are fighting for their liberty in defending our own.

BENJAMIN FRANKLIN, STATESMAN AND SCIENTIST

The history of America is now the central feature of the history of the world.

THEODORE ROOSEVELT, 26TH PRESIDENT (1901–1909)

Guard against the impostures of pretended patriotism.
GEORGE WASHINGTON, 1ST PRESIDENT (1789–1797)

....

A man's country is not a certain area of land, of mountains, rivers, and woods, but it is a principle and patriotism is loyalty to that principle.

GEORGE WILLIAM CURTIS, AUTHOR AND EDITOR

....

A fine genius in his own country is like gold in the mine.
BENJAMIN FRANKLIN, STATESMAN AND SCIENTIST

When an American says that he loves his country, he means not only that he loves the New England hills, the prairies glistening in the sun, the wide and rising plains, the great mountains, and the sea. He means that he loves an inner air, an inner light in which freedom lives and in which a man can draw the breath of self-respect.
ADLAI STEVENSON, FORMER GOVERNOR OF ILLINOIS AND DIPLOMAT

This country, with its institutions, belongs to the people who inhabit it.
ABRAHAM LINCOLN, 16TH PRESIDENT (1861–1865)

Patriotism means we share a single country. In all our diversity, each of us has a bond with every other American.

GEORGE W. BUSH, 43RD PRESIDENT (2001–)

America will remain strong and united, but its strength will remain dedicated to the safety and sanity of the entire family of man, as well as to our own precious freedom.

GERALD R. FORD, 38TH PRESIDENT (1974–1977)

Yesterday the greatest question was decided which ever was debated in America; and a greater perhaps never was, nor will be, decided among men. A resolution was passed without one dissenting colony, "that these United Colonies are, and of right ought to be, free and independent States."

JOHN ADAMS, 1ST VICE PRESIDENT (1789–1797) AND 2ND PRESIDENT (1797–1801)

It is time for us to realize that we're too great a nation to limit ourselves to small dreams.

RONALD REAGAN, 40TH PRESIDENT (1981–1989)

....

These are the United States—a united people with a united purpose.

LYNDON B. JOHNSON, 36TH PRESIDENT (1963–1969)

The message of the United States is a spiritual message, a statement of high ideals and perseverance in their achievement. It is the message of human dignity; it is the message of the freedom of ideas, speech, press.

LYNDON B. JOHNSON, 36TH PRESIDENT (1963–1969)

This nation has placed its destiny in the hands and heads of its millions of free men and women; and its faith in freedom under the guidance of God.

FRANKLIN DELANO ROOSEVELT, 32ND PRESIDENT (1933–1945)

America is much more than a geographical fact. It is a political and moral fact—the first community in which men set out in principle to institutionalize freedom, responsible government, and human equality.

ADLAI STEVENSON, FORMER GOVERNOR OF ILLINOIS AND DIPLOMAT

America is great not because of what she has done for herself, but because of what she has done for others.

JOHN MCCAIN, U.S. SENATOR

Our nation is the greatest force for good in history—and we show our gratitude by doing our duty.

GEORGE W. BUSH, 43RD PRESIDENT (2001–   )

When the Lord calls me home, when-ever that may be, I will leave the greatest love for this country of ours and eternal optimism for its future.

RONALD REAGAN, 40TH PRESIDENT (1981–1989)

....

With malice toward none, with charity for all, with firmness in the right as God gives us to see the right, let us strive on to finish the work we are in, to bind up the nation's wounds.

ABRAHAM LINCOLN, 16TH PRESIDENT (1861–1865)

PEACE

—⭐—

Confident and unafraid, we labor on—not toward a strategy of annihilation but toward a strategy of peace.

JOHN F. KENNEDY, 35TH PRESIDENT (1961–1963)

A steadfast concert for peace can never be maintained except by a partnership of democratic nations.

WOODROW WILSON, 28TH PRESIDENT (1913–1921)

We welcome change and openness; for we believe that freedom and security go together, that the advance of human liberty can only strengthen the cause of world peace.

RONALD REAGAN, 40TH PRESIDENT (1981–1989)

I am proud of the fact that I never invented weapons to kill.

THOMAS EDISON, Inventor

We have known the bitterness of defeat and the exultation of triumph, and from both we have learned there can be no turning back. We must go forward to preserve in peace what we won in war.

GENERAL DOUGLAS MACARTHUR

Conflicts are created, conducted, and sustained by human beings. They can be ended by human beings.

GEORGE MITCHELL, FORMER U.S. SENATOR MAJORITY LEADER

We must teach our children to resolve their conflicts with words, not weapons.

WILLIAM J. CLINTON, 42ND PRESIDENT (1993–2001)

I like to believe that people in the long run are going to do more to promote peace than our governments. Indeed, I think that people want peace so much that one of these days governments had better get out of the way and let them have it.

DWIGHT D. EISENHOWER, 34TH PRESIDENT (1953–1961)

When you can whip any man in the world, you never know peace.

MUHAMMAD ALI, FORMER WORLD HEAVYWEIGHT CHAMPION

....

Don't confuse being "soft" with seeing the other guy's point of view.

GEORGE H.W. BUSH, 41ST PRESIDENT (1989–1993)

....

There never was a time when, in my opinion, some way could not be found to prevent the drawing of the sword.

ULYSSES S. GRANT, 18TH PRESIDENT (1869–1877)

Nonviolence is a powerful and just weapon. It is a weapon unique in history, which cuts without wounding and ennobles the man who wields it. It is a sword that heals.

MARTIN LUTHER KING, JR., CIVIL RIGHTS LEADER

....

Enduring peace cannot be bought at the cost of other people's freedom.

FRANKLIN DELANO ROOSEVELT, 32ND PRESIDENT (1933–1945)

....

Mankind will never win lasting peace so long as men use their full resources only in tasks of war. While we are yet at peace, let us mobilize the potentialities, particularly the moral and spiritual potentialities, which we usually reserve for war.

JOHN FOSTER DULLES, FORMER SECRETARY OF STATE

A world that begins to witness the rebirth of trust among nations can find its way to a peace that is neither partial nor punitive.

DWIGHT D. EISENHOWER, 34TH PRESIDENT (1953–1961)

I realize that the pursuit of peace is not as dramatic as the pursuit of war—and frequently the words of the pursuer fall on deaf ears.

JOHN F. KENNEDY, 35TH PRESIDENT (1961–1963)

Let us be united for peace. Let us also be united against defeat.

RICHARD M. NIXON, 37TH PRESIDENT (1969–1974)

The great objects of our pursuit as a people are best to be attained by peace, and are entirely consistent with the tranquillity and interests of the rest of mankind.

FRANKLIN PIERCE, 14TH PRESIDENT (1853–1857)

You don't have to have fought in a war to love peace.

GERALDINE FERRARO, 1984 DEMOCRATIC VICE PRESIDENTIAL NOMINEE

It will be our wish and purpose that the processes of peace shall be absolutely open and that they shall involve and permit henceforth no secret understandings of any kind.

WOODROW WILSON, 28TH PRESIDENT (1913–1921)

The springs of human conflict cannot be eradicated through institutions but only through the reform of the individual human being.

GENERAL DOUGLAS MACARTHUR

It must be peace without victory. ... Only a peace between equals can last.
WOODROW WILSON, 28TH PRESIDENT (1913–1921)

Let us all understand that the question before us is not whether some Americans are for peace and some Americans are against peace. ... The great question is: How can we win America's peace?
RICHARD M. NIXON, 37TH PRESIDENT (1969–1974)

Our goal is not the victory of might, but the vindication of right—not peace at the expense of freedom, but both peace and freedom.
JOHN F. KENNEDY, 35TH PRESIDENT (1961–1963)

We seek peace, knowing that peace is the climate of freedom.
DWIGHT D. EISENHOWER, 34TH PRESIDENT (1953–1961)

You have to take chances for peace, just as you must take chances in war. ... The ability to get to the verge without getting into the war is the necessary art. If you try to run away from it, if you are scared to go to the brink, you are lost.
JOHN FOSTER DULLES, FORMER SECRETARY OF STATE

....

The real and lasting victories are those of peace and not of war.

RALPH WALDO EMERSON, POET AND ESSAYIST

It is impossible, my countrymen, to speak of peace without profound emotion. In thousands of homes in America, in millions of homes around the world, there are vacant chairs. It would be a shameful confession of our unworthiness if it should develop that we have abandoned the hope for which all these men died. Surely civilization is old enough, surely mankind is mature enough so that we ought in our own lifetime to find a way to permanent peace.

HERBERT HOOVER, 31ST PRESIDENT (1929–1933)

Even peace may be purchased at too high a price.

BENJAMIN FRANKLIN, STATESMAN AND SCIENTIST

Peace, above all things, is to be desired, but blood must sometimes be spilled to obtain it on equitable and lasting terms.

ANDREW JACKSON, 7TH PRESIDENT (1829–1837)

If man does find the solution for world peace it will be the most revolutionary reversal of his record we have ever known.

GENERAL DOUGLAS MACARTHUR

We will guard against violence, knowing it strikes from our hands the very weapons which we seek—progress, obedience to the law, and belief in American values.

LYNDON B. JOHNSON, 36TH PRESIDENT (1963–1969)

Though force can protect in emergency, only justice, fairness, consideration and cooperation can finally lead men to the dawn of eternal peace.

DWIGHT D. EISENHOWER, 34TH PRESIDENT (1953–1961)

No man should think that peace comes easily. Peace does not come by merely wanting it, or shouting for it, or marching down Main Street for it. Peace is built brick by brick, mortared by the stubborn effort and the total energy and imagination of able and dedicated men. And it is built in the living faith that, in the end, man can and will master his own destiny.

LYNDON B. JOHNSON, 36TH PRESIDENT (1963–1969)

Our first, our greatest, our most relentless purpose is peace. For without peace there is nothing.

ADLAI STEVENSON, FORMER GOVERNOR OF ILLINOIS AND DIPLOMAT

We must complete a structure of peace, so that it will be said of this generation—our generation of Americans—by the people of all nations, not only that we ended one war but that we prevented future wars.

RICHARD M. NIXON, 37TH PRESIDENT (1969–1974)

Peace is not merely a distant goal that we seek, but a means by which we arrive at that goal.

MARTIN LUTHER KING, JR., CIVIL RIGHTS LEADER

Peace is not made at the council table or by treaties, but in the hearts of men.

HERBERT HOOVER, 31ST PRESIDENT (1929–1933)

World peace, like community peace, does not require that each man love his neighbor—it requires only that they live together with mutual tolerance, submitting their disputes to a just and peaceful settlement.

JOHN F. KENNEDY, 35TH PRESIDENT (1961–1963)

....

It isn't enough to talk about peace. One must believe in it. And it isn't enough to believe in it. One must work at it.

ELEANOR ROOSEVELT, FORMER FIRST LADY

....

The soldier above all others prays for peace, for it is the soldier who must suffer and bear the deepest wounds and scars of war.

GENERAL DOUGLAS MACARTHUR

The example of America must be the example not merely of peace because it will not fight, but of peace because peace is the healing and elevating influence of the world, and strife is not. There is such a thing as a man being too proud to fight. There is such a thing as a nation being so right that it does not need to convince others by force that it is right.

WOODROW WILSON, 28TH PRESIDENT (1913–1921)

There can be no greater good than the quest for peace, and no finer purpose than the preservation of freedom.

RONALD REAGAN, 40TH PRESIDENT (1981–1989)

I speak of peace as the necessary rational end of rational men.

JOHN F. KENNEDY, 35TH PRESIDENT (1961–1963)

The best way to destroy an enemy is to make him a friend.

ABRAHAM LINCOLN, 16TH PRESIDENT (1861–1865)

The hunger for peace is too great, the hour in history too late, for any government to mock men's hopes with mere words and promises and gestures.

DWIGHT D. EISENHOWER, 34TH PRESIDENT (1953–1961)

Peace is a journey of a thousand miles and it must be taken one step at a time.

LYNDON B. JOHNSON, 36TH PRESIDENT (1963–1969)

....

To be prepared for war is one of the most effectual ways of preserving peace.

GEORGE WASHINGTON, 1ST PRESIDENT (1789–1797)

....

The greatest honor history can bestow is that of peacemaker.

RICHARD M. NIXON, 37TH PRESIDENT (1969–1974)

There must be, not a balance of power, but a community of power; not organized rivalries, but an organization of common peace.

WOODROW WILSON, 28TH PRESIDENT (1913–1921)

....

Man must evolve for all human conflict a method which rejects revenge, aggression and retaliation. The foundation of such a method is love.

MARTIN LUTHER KING, JR., CIVIL RIGHTS LEADER

....

What has violence ever accomplished? What has it ever created? No martyr's cause has ever been stilled by an assassin's bullet.

ROBERT F. KENNEDY, FORMER ATTORNEY GENERAL AND U.S. SENATOR

Non-violence leads to the highest ethics, which is the goal of all evolution. Until we stop harming all other living beings, we are still savages.

THOMAS EDISON, INVENTOR

Peace is not something you wish for; it's something you make, something you do, something you are, and something you give away.

ROBERT FULGHUM, UNITARIAN CLERGYMAN AND AUTHOR

As a rule, they who preach by word or deed "peace at any price" are not possessed of anything worth having, and are oblivious to the interest of others including their own dependents.

GENERAL DOUGLAS MACARTHUR

Let us examine our attitude toward peace itself. Too many of us think it is impossible. Too many think it unreal. But that is a dangerous, defeatist attitude.

JOHN F. KENNEDY, 35TH PRESIDENT (1961–1963)

....

I say we are going to have peace even if we have to fight for it.

DWIGHT D. EISENHOWER, 34TH PRESIDENT (1953–1961)

....

The pursuit of peace resembles the building of a great cathedral. It is the work of a generation. In concept it requires a master architect; in execution, the labors of many.

HUBERT HUMPHREY, 38TH VICE PRESIDENT (1965–1969)

POLITICS

———★———

All of us, despite the differences that enliven our politics, are united in the one big idea that freedom is our birthright and its defense is always our first responsibility.

JOHN MCCAIN, U.S. SENATOR

The American people need no course in philosophy or political science or church history to know that God should not be made into a celestial party chairman.

MARIO CUOMO, FORMER GOVERNOR OF NEW YORK

No matter how honest and decent we are in our private lives, if we do not have the right kind of law and the right kind of administration of the law, we cannot go forward as a nation.

THEODORE ROOSEVELT, 26TH PRESIDENT (1901–1909)

America has two great dominant strands of political thought—conservatism, which, at its very best, draws lines that should not be crossed; and progressivism, which, at it's very best, breaks down barriers that are no longer needed or should never have been erected in the first place.

WILLIAM J. CLINTON, 42ND PRESIDENT (1993–2001)

All people are born alike—except Republicans and Democrats.

GROUCHO MARX, COMEDIAN

I am more than ever convinced that whatever our private political views, the great majority of us check our more obvious prejudices at the door.

PETER JENNINGS, BROADCAST JOURNALIST

We do not need another slogan.

JIMMY CARTER, 39TH PRESIDENT (1977–1981)

People talk about the middle of the road as though it were unacceptable. Actually, all human problems, excepting morals, come into the gray areas. Things are not all black and white. There have to be compromises. The middle of the road is all of the usable surface. The extremes, right and left, are in the gutters.

DWIGHT D. EISENHOWER, 34TH PRESIDENT (1953–1961)

....

Politics is war, without bullets and shells—usually.

COLIN POWELL, FORMER SECRETARY OF STATE

....

Knowledge of human nature is the beginning and end of political education.

HENRY ADAMS, HISTORIAN AND AUTHOR

Here we are the way politics ought to be in America; the politics of happiness, the politics of purpose and the politics of joy.

HUBERT HUMPHREY, 38TH VICE PRESIDENT (1965–1969)

....

Politics is an act of faith; you have to show some kind of confidence in the intellectual and moral capacity of the public.

GEORGE MCGOVERN, FORMER U.S. SENATOR

....

After lots of people who go into politics have been in it for a while they find that to stay in politics they have to make all sorts of compromises to satisfy their supporters and that it becomes awfully important for them to keep their jobs because they have nowhere else to go.

ADLAI STEVENSON, FORMER GOVERNOR OF ILLINOIS AND DIPLOMAT

If our political institutions were perfect, they would absolutely prevent the political domination of money in any part of our affairs.

THEODORE ROOSEVELT, 26TH PRESIDENT (1901–1909)

Politics is the business of men. I don' care what offices they hold, or who supports them. I care only about people.

DOLLY TODD MADISON, FORMER FIRST LADY

It is hard to penetrate the modern feeling—and I understand why they feel it—that politics is about special interests, that it's corrupt, that it's not really after these large goals that it was when we were there.

DORIS KEARNS GOODWIN, PH.D., PULITZER PRIZE-WINNING HISTORIAN

Politics is supposed to be the second oldest profession. I have come to realize that it bears a very close resemblance to the first.

RONALD REAGAN, 40TH PRESIDENT (1981–1989)

Our founders were insightful students of human nature. They feared the abuse of power because they understood that every human being has not only "better angels" in his nature, but also an innate vulnerability to temptation—especially the temptation to abuse power over others.

AL GORE, 45TH VICE PRESIDENT (1993–2001)

....

There is nothing political about human decency.

THOMAS DEWEY, FORMER GOVERNOR OF NEW YORK

....

True liberalism is a force truly of the spirit, a force proceeding from the deep realization that economic freedom cannot be sacrificed if political freedom is to be preserved.

HERBERT HOOVER, 31ST PRESIDENT (1929–1933)

That flag doesn't belong to any president. It doesn't belong to any ideology and it doesn't belong to any political party. It belongs to all the American people.

JOHN KERRY, U.S. SENATOR

A broken promise is bad enough in private life. It is worse in the field of politics.

THEODORE ROOSEVELT, 26TH PRESIDENT (1901–1909)

Politics is the art of looking for trouble, finding it everywhere, diagnosing it incorrectly and applying the wrong remedies.

GROUCHO MARX, COMEDIAN

The public life of every political figure is a continual struggle to rescue an element of choice from the pressure of circumstance.

HENRY KISSINGER, FOREIGN-POLICY ADVISER

Of all the dispositions and habits which lead to political prosperity, religion and morality are indispensable supports.

GEORGE WASHINGTON, 1ST PRESIDENT (1789–1797)

The more you read and observe about this politics thing, you got to admit that each party is worse than the other. The one that's out always looks the best.

WILL ROGERS, HUMORIST AND ACTOR

There are times in politics when you must be on the right side and lose.

JOHN KENNETH GALBRAITH, ECONOMIST AND POLITICAL ADVISOR

POWER

—★—

One of the great strengths of America, and the reason we are held in such high regard throughout the world, is that people trust our power, and they trust the way in which we use our power. The more powerful you are, the more people want to trust you with that power. They would hate to not trust you with that power.

COLIN POWELL, FORMER SECRETARY OF STATE

Power must never be trusted without a check.

JOHN ADAMS, 1ST VICE PRESIDENT (1789–1797) AND 2ND PRESIDENT (1797–1801)

Power should not be concentrated in the hands of so few, and powerlessness in the hands of so many.

MAGGIE KUHN, SOCIAL ACTIVIST AND AUTHOR

Speech is power: speech is to persuade, to convert, to compel.

RALPH WALDO EMERSON, POET AND ESSAYIST

Power can be taken, but not given. The process of the taking is empowerment in itself.

GLORIA STEINEM, EDITOR, WRITER, AND FEMINIST

Abuse of power isn't limited to bad guys in other nations. It happens in our own country if we're not vigilant.

CLINT EASTWOOD, ACTOR, DIRECTOR, AND PRODUCER

Nearly all men can stand adversity, but if you want to test a man's character, give him power.

ABRAHAM LINCOLN, 16TH PRESIDENT (1861–1865)

Americans distrust concepts like the International Criminal Court, and claims by the UN to be the "sole source of legitimacy" for the use of force, because Americans have a profound distrust of accumulated power.

JESSE HELMS, FORMER U.S. SENATOR

....

I hope our wisdom will grow with our power, and teach us that the less we use our power the greater it will be.

THOMAS JEFFERSON, 3RD PRESIDENT (1801–1809)

....

All power is limited by definite boundaries and laws. No power is absolute, infinite, unbridled, arbitrary, and lawless. Every power is bound to laws, right, and equity.

MADELEINE ALBRIGHT, FORMER SECRETARY OF STATE

Our natural distrust of concentrated power and our devotion to openness and democracy are what have lead us as a people to consistently choose good over evil in our collective aspirations more than the people any other nation.

AL GORE, 45TH VICE PRESIDENT (1993–2001)

Liberty may be endangered by the abuse of liberty, but also by the abuse of power.

JAMES MADISON, 4TH PRESIDENT (1809–1817)

Unless you choose to do great things with it, it makes no difference how much you are rewarded, or how much power you have.

OPRAH WINFREY, TELEVISION TALK-SHOW HOST, ACTRESS, AND PRODUCER

....

Power descends from knowledge.

MADELEINE ALBRIGHT, FORMER SECRETARY OF STATE

....

Power in defense of freedom is greater than power in behalf of tyranny and oppression.

MALCOLM X, MUSLIM LEADER

We do not use American power to establish empire. We do not spend our blood and treasure for territorial gain, nor for oil, nor to enrich our corporations. ... Our power must be directed in ways that bolster freedom, democracy, economic prosperity, international institutions and rules.

JOHN MCCAIN, U.S. SENATOR

THE PRESIDENCY

Everybody wants to tell the president what to do, and boy, he needs to be told many times.

RICHARD M. NIXON, 37TH PRESIDENT (1969–1974)

For the trust reposed in me I will return the courage and the devotion that befit the time. I can do no less.

FRANKLIN DELANO ROOSEVELT, 32ND PRESIDENT (1933–1945)

I believe it is the job of a president to understand and explain the time in which he serves, to set forth a vision of where we need to go and a strategy of how to get there, and then to pursue it with all his mind and heart.

WILLIAM J. CLINTON, 42ND PRESIDENT (1993–2001)

I seek the presidency to build a better America. It's that simple—that big.

GEORGE H.W. BUSH, 41ST PRESIDENT (1989–1993)

An assassin's bullet has thrust upon me the awesome burden of the Presidency.

LYNDON B. JOHNSON, 36TH PRESIDENT (1963–1969), ON THE ASSASSINATION OF PRESIDENT JOHN F. KENNEDY

No President who performs his duties faithfully and conscientiously can have any leisure.

JAMES POLK, 11TH PRESIDENT (1845–1849)

I am acutely aware that you have not elected me as your President by your ballots, and so I ask you to confirm me as your President with your prayers.

GERALD R. FORD, 38TH PRESIDENT (1974–1977), ON THE RESIGNATION OF PRESIDENT RICHARD M. NIXON

Your trust is what gives a President his powers of leadership and his personal strength.

RONALD REAGAN, 40TH PRESIDENT (1981–1989)

All the president is, is a glorified public relations man who spends his time flattering, kissing, and kicking people to get them to do what they are supposed to do anyway.

HARRY S. TRUMAN, 33RD PRESIDENT (1945–1953)

The presidency is more than a popularity contest.

AL GORE, 45TH VICE PRESIDENT (1993–2001)

With America's sons in the fields far away ... I do not believe that I should devote an hour or a day of my time to any personal partisan causes or to any duties other than the awesome duties of this office—the Presidency of your country.

LYNDON B. JOHNSON, 36TH PRESIDENT (1963–1969), ON ANNOUNCING HE WILL NOT SEEK RE-ELECTION

When I was a boy I was told that anybody could become President; I'm beginning to believe it.

CLARENCE DARROW, LAWYER AND PUBLIC SPEAKER

....

Any man who wants to be president is either an egomaniac or crazy.

DWIGHT D. EISENHOWER, 34TH PRESIDENT (1953–1961)

....

There's an inescapable bond that binds together all who have lived in the White House. Though we hail from different backgrounds and ideologies, we are singularly unique, even eternally bound, by our common devotion and service to this wonderful country.

GEORGE H.W. BUSH, 41ST PRESIDENT (1989–1993)

Democracy means that anyone can grow up to be president, and anyone who doesn't grow up can be vice president.

JOHNNY CARSON, ENTERTAINER

PROGRESS

---★---

It's the repetition of affirmations that leads to belief. And once that belief becomes a deep conviction, things begin to happen.

MUHAMMAD ALI, FORMER WORLD HEAVYWEIGHT CHAMPION

Often, progress will come in small, quiet steps, less dramatic than the toppling of statues. Occasional setbacks are inevitable. But these efforts are vitally important and they are an essential element of the war on global terror.

CONDOLEEZZA RICE, SECRETARY OF STATE AND FORMER NATIONAL SECURITY ADVISOR

There are no great limits to growth because there are no limits of human intelligence, imagination, and wonder.

RONALD REAGAN, 40TH PRESIDENT (1981–1989)

In your hands, my fellow citizens, more than mine, will rest the final success or failure of our course.

JOHN F. KENNEDY, 35TH PRESIDENT (1961–1963)

The race is more important than the individual. Because we are a social animal, and that's the nature of social animals.

ADMIRAL ALAN SHEPARD, JR., ASTRONAUT

America has believed that in differentiation, not in uniformity, lies the path of progress. It acted on this belief; it has advanced human happiness, and it has prospered.

LOUIS BRANDEIS, FORMER U.S. SUPREME COURT ASSOCIATE JUSTICE

No matter whether the original goal was set too high or too low, our objective is quicker and better results.

FRANKLIN DELANO ROOSEVELT, 32ND PRESIDENT (1933–1945)

....

That's one small step for man, one giant leap for mankind.

NEIL ARMSTRONG, ASTRONAUT

....

Since the course of progress is rarely a straight line you will often need a compass to guide and focus your courage.

GENERAL HENRY H. SHELTON, FORMER CHAIRMAN OF THE JOINT CHIEFS OF STAFF

Laws and institutions must go hand in hand with the progress of the human mind. As that becomes more developed, more enlightened, as new discoveries are made, new truths disclosed, and manners and opinions change with the change of circumstances, institutions must advance also, and keep pace with the times.

THOMAS JEFFERSON, 3RD PRESIDENT (1801–1809)

There are risks and costs to a program of action. But they are far less than the long-range risks and costs of comfortable inaction.

JOHN F. KENNEDY, 35TH PRESIDENT (1961–1963)

Don't find fault, find a remedy.

HENRY FORD, INDUSTRIALIST AND AUTOMOBILE MANUFACTURER

If there is no struggle, there is no progress. Those who profess to favor freedom, and yet deprecate agitation, are men who want crops without plowing the ground.

FREDERICK DOUGLASS, ABOLITIONIST AND AUTOBIOGRAPHER

Restlessness and discontent are the first necessities of progress.

THOMAS EDISON, INVENTOR

....

Progress is the activity of today and the assurance of tomorrow.

RALPH WALDO EMERSON, POET AND ESSAYIST

....

Amidst all the clutter, beyond all the obstacles, aside from all the static, are the goals set. Put your head down, do the best job possible, let the flak pass, and work towards those goals.

DONALD RUMSFELD, U.S. SECRETARY OF DEFENSE

If you wait for inspiration, inspiration's going to go away and look for more fertile ground to work with.

RITA DOVE, FORMER U.S. POET LAUREATE

Since the beginning of our American history, we have been engaged in change— in a perpetual peaceful revolution.

FRANKLIN DELANO ROOSEVELT, 32ND PRESIDENT (1933–1945)

We cannot solve today's problems using the mindset that created them.

ALBERT EINSTEIN, NOBEL PRIZE-WINNING PHYSICIST

So many of the major steps forward in our society's progress started with just a handful of people.

RALPH NADER, THIRD-PARTY PRESIDENTIAL NOMINEE

Humanity is acquiring all the right technology for all the wrong reasons.

R. BUCKMINSTER FULLER, ARCHITECT AND ENGINEER

A united determination to do is worth more than divided counsels upon the method of doing.

ULYSSES S. GRANT, 18TH PRESIDENT (1869–1877)

Even a mistake may turn out to be the one thing necessary to a worthwhile achievement.

HENRY FORD, INDUSTRIALIST AND AUTOMOBILE MANUFACTURER

The truth is: Change is tough. There is enormous institutional pressure in our country against change.

HOWARD DEAN, FORMER GOVERNOR OF VERMONT

Embedded in democracy is the idea of progress. Democracy addresses injustice and corrects it. The progress is not automatic. It requires a sustained exercise of political will.

ANTHONY M. KENNEDY, U.S. SUPREME COURT ASSOCIATE JUSTICE

If we intend to be a society that's going to be rich for our children, we've got to explore.

DANIEL S. GOLDIN, FORMER NASA ADMINISTRATOR

Time and tide wait for no man. A pompous and self-satisfied proverb, and was true for a billion years; but in our day of electric wires and water-ballast we turn it around: Man waits not for time nor tide.

MARK TWAIN, AUTHOR AND HUMORIST

Human progress never rolls in on wheels of inevitability; it comes through the tireless efforts of men willing to be co-workers with God, and without this hard work, time itself becomes an ally of the forces of social stagnation. We must use time creatively, in the knowledge that the time is always ripe to do right.

MARTIN LUTHER KING, JR., CIVIL RIGHTS LEADER

He who is firmly seated in authority soon learns to think security, and not progress, the highest lesson of statecraft.

JAMES RUSSELL LOWELL, POET, EDITOR, AND DIPLOMAT

The country needs and, unless I mistake its temper, the country demands bold, persistent experimentation. It is common sense to take a method and try it; if it fails, admit it frankly and try another. But above all try something.

FRANKLIN DELANO ROOSEVELT, 32ND PRESIDENT (1933–1945)

....

We've always believed in something called progress. We've always had a faith that the days of our children would be better than our own.

JIMMY CARTER, 39TH PRESIDENT (1977–1981)

Conformity is the jailer of freedom and the enemy of growth.

JOHN F. KENNEDY, 35TH PRESIDENT (1961–1963)

People should think things out fresh and not just accept conventional terms
and the conventional way of doing things.

R. BUCKMINSTER FULLER, ARCHITECT AND ENGINEER

Failure is simply the opportunity to begin again, this time more intelligently.

HENRY FORD, INDUSTRIALIST AND AUTOMOBILE MANUFACTURER

All progress has resulted from people who took unpopular positions.

ADLAI STEVENSON, FORMER GOVERNOR OF ILLINOIS

Quality of Life

———— ★ ————

This country will not be a good place for any of us to live in unless we make it a good place for all of us to live in.

THEODORE ROOSEVELT, 26TH PRESIDENT (1901–1909)

We in this country are committed to narrowing the gap between promise and performance … between opportunity for the well-to-do and opportunity for the poor, between education for the successful and education for the whole people.

ADLAI STEVENSON, FORMER GOVERNOR OF ILLINOIS AND DIPLOMAT

Turning our eyes to other nations, our great desire is to see our brethren of the human race secured in the blessings enjoyed by ourselves, and advancing in knowledge, in freedom, and in social happiness.

ANDREW JACKSON, 7TH PRESIDENT (1829–1837)

Where justice is denied, where poverty is enforced, where ignorance prevails, and where any one class is made to feel that society is in an organized conspiracy to oppress, rob, and degrade them, neither persons nor property will be safe.

FREDERICK DOUGLASS, ABOLITIONIST AND AUTOBIOGRAPHER

Not all of our people are happy and prosperous; not all of them are virtuous and law-abiding. But on the whole the opportunities offered to the individual to secure the comforts of life are better than are found elsewhere and largely better than they were here one hundred years ago.

BENJAMIN HARRISON, 23RD PRESIDENT (1889–1893)

....

I am proud of America, and I am proud to be an American. Life will be a little better here for my children than for me.

GERALD R. FORD, 38TH PRESIDENT (1974–1977)

....

If a free society cannot help the many who are poor, it cannot save the few who are rich.

JOHN F. KENNEDY, 35TH PRESIDENT (1961–1963)

I have the audacity to believe that people everywhere can have three meals a day for their bodies, education and culture for their minds, and dignity, quality, and freedom for their spirits. I believe that what self-centered men have torn down, other-centered men can build up.

MARTIN LUTHER KING, JR., CIVIL RIGHTS LEADER

We are poor indeed if this Nation cannot afford to lift from every recess of American life the dread fear of the unemployed that they are not needed in the world.

FRANKLIN DELANO ROOSEVELT, 32ND PRESIDENT (1933–1945)

The Great Society is a place where every child can find knowledge to enrich his mind and to enlarge his talents. ... It is a place where the city of man serves not only the needs of the body and the demands of commerce but the desire for beauty and the hunger for community. ... It is a place where men are more concerned with the quality of their goals than the quantity of their goods.

LYNDON B. JOHNSON, 36TH PRESIDENT (1963–1969)

No person is your friend who demands your silence, or denies your right to grow.

ALICE WALKER, AUTHOR

Here in America we are fortunate that most of our people have not only the blessings of liberty but also the means to live full and good, and by the world's standards even abundant, lives.

RICHARD M. NIXON, 37TH PRESIDENT (1969–1974)

The American people desire, and are determined to work for, a world in which all nations and all peoples are free to govern themselves as they see fit, and to achieve a decent and satisfying life. Above all else, our people desire, and are determined to work for, peace on earth—a just and lasting peace—based on genuine agreement freely arrived at by equals.

HARRY S. TRUMAN, 33RD PRESIDENT (1945–1953)

The beauty of a democracy is that you never can tell when a youngster is born what he is going to do with himself, and that no matter how humbly he is born, no matter where he is born, no matter what circumstances hamper him at the outset, he has got a chance to master the minds and lead the imaginations of the whole country.

WOODROW WILSON, 28TH PRESIDENT (1913–1921)

Every gun that is made, every warship launched, every rocket fired, signifies in the final sense a theft from those who hunger and are not fed, those who are cold and are not clothed.

DWIGHT D. EISENHOWER, 34TH PRESIDENT (1953–1961)

I believe that, as long as there is plenty, poverty is evil.

ROBERT F. KENNEDY, FORMER ATTORNEY GENERAL

Sacrifice

———★———

In the long history of the world, only a few generations have been granted the role of defending freedom in its hour of maximum danger.

John F. Kennedy, 35th President (1961–1963)

I have lived—daily and nightly—with the cost of war. I know the pain that it has inflicted. I know, perhaps better than anyone, the misgivings that it has aroused.

Lyndon B. Johnson, 36th President (1963–1969)

The soldier, above all other men, is required to practice the greatest act of religious training—sacrifice.

General Douglas MacArthur

A man must be willing to die for justice. Death is an inescapable reality and men die daily, but good deeds live forever.

Jesse Jackson, Civil Rights Leader

My fellow Americans, a tree takes a long time to grow, and wounds take a long time to heal. But we must begin. Those who are lost now belong to God. Some day we will be with them. But until that happens, their legacy must be our lives.

William J. Clinton, 42nd President (1993–2001), On the Oklahoma City Bombing

Men may die, but the fabrics of free institutions remains unshaken.

CHESTER A. ARTHUR, 21ST PRESIDENT (1881–1885)

....

The sacrifices borne in our defense are not shared equally by all Americans.

JOHN MCCAIN, U.S. SENATOR

....

If a man hasn't discovered something that he will die for, he isn't fit to live.

MARTIN LUTHER KING, JR., CIVIL RIGHTS LEADER

We will never forget them, nor the last time we saw them … as they prepared for their journey and waved goodbye and "slipped the surly bonds of earth" to "touch the face of God."

RONALD REAGAN, 40TH PRESIDENT (1981–1989), ON THE LOSS OF THE CHALLENGER CREW

It is rather for us to be here dedicated to the great task remaining before us— that from these honored dead we take increased devotion to that cause for which they gave the last full measure of devotion—that we here highly resolve that these dead shall not have died in vain, that this nation under God shall have a new birth of freedom, and that government of the people, by the people, for the people shall not perish from the earth.

ABRAHAM LINCOLN, 16TH PRESIDENT (1861–1865), ON THE BATTLE OF GETTYSBURG

But let men everywhere know, however, that a strong, a confident, and a vigilant America stands ready tonight to seek an honorable peace—and stands ready tonight to defend an honored cause whatever the price, whatever the burden, whatever the sacrifice that duty may require.

LYNDON B. JOHNSON, 36TH PRESIDENT (1963–1969)

Only free peoples can hold their purpose and their honor steady to a common end and prefer the interest of mankind to any narrow interest of their own.

WOODROW WILSON, 28TH PRESIDENT (1913–1921)

In the face of death, let us honor life.

WILLIAM J. CLINTON, 42ND PRESIDENT (1993–2001)

And the whole idea of being willing to risk one's life for achievement—I say that's an honorable attitude.

ADMIRAL ALAN SHEPARD, JR., ASTRONAUT

....

The graves of young Americans who answered the call to service surround the globe.

JOHN F. KENNEDY, 35TH PRESIDENT (1961–1963)

Of those to whom much is given, much is asked. I cannot say and no man could say that no more will be asked of us.

LYNDON B. JOHNSON, 36TH PRESIDENT (1963–1969)

We desire no conquest, no dominion. We seek no indemnities for ourselves, no material compensation for the sacrifices we shall cheerfully make. We are but one of the champions of the rights of mankind. We shall be satisfied when those rights have been made as secure as the faith and the freedom of nations can make them.

WOODROW WILSON, 28TH PRESIDENT (1913–1921)

Giving back involves a certain amount of giving up.

COLIN POWELL, FORMER SECRETARY OF STATE

....

If there must be trouble let it be in my day that my child may have peace.

THOMAS PAINE, AMERICAN REVOLUTIONARY

....

Every step toward the goal of justice requires sacrifice, suffering, and struggle; the tireless exertions and passionate concern of dedicated individuals.

MARTIN LUTHER KING, JR., CIVIL RIGHTS LEADER

SECURITY

---★---

In this young century, our world needs a new definition of security. Our security is not merely found in spheres of influence, or some balance of power. The security of our world is found in the advancing rights of mankind.

GEORGE W. BUSH, 43RD PRESIDENT (2001–   )

We will bankrupt ourselves in the vain search for absolute security.

DWIGHT D. EISENHOWER, 34TH PRESIDENT (1953–1961)

The central challenge for us today is to our steadfastedness of purpose. We are no longer tempted by isolationism. But we must also learn to deal effectively with the contradictions of the world, the need to cooperate with potential adversaries without euphoria, without undermining our determination to compete with such adversaries and if necessary confront the threats they may pose to our security.

JIMMY CARTER, 39TH PRESIDENT (1977–1981)

Neither the United States of America nor the world community of nations can tolerate deliberate deception and offensive threats on the part of any nation, large or small.

JOHN F. KENNEDY, 35TH PRESIDENT (1961–1963)

Our hope—our determination—is nothing less than this: to live our lives confident that we are safe at home and secure in our world.

JOHN KERRY, U.S. SENATOR

....

I will not yield; I will not rest; I will not relent in waging this struggle for freedom and security for the American people.

GEORGE W. BUSH, 43RD PRESIDENT (2001–   )

....

There are threats now to our freedom, indeed to our very existence, that other generations could never even have imagined.

RONALD REAGAN, 40TH PRESIDENT (1981–1989)

Our nation's security lies in the strength of our people—our people at work, in prosperous communities, in sound mental and physical heath.

LYNDON B. JOHNSON, 36TH PRESIDENT (1963–1969)

Our arms must be mighty, ready for instant action, so that no potential aggressor may be tempted to risk his own destruction.

DWIGHT D. EISENHOWER, 34TH PRESIDENT (1953–1961)

Every nation that would preserve its tranquility, its riches, its independence, and its self-respect must keep alive its martial ardor and be at all times prepared to defend itself.

GENERAL DOUGLAS MACARTHUR

The man who trades freedom for security does not deserve nor will he ever receive either.

BENJAMIN FRANKLIN, STATESMAN AND SCIENTIST

The Nation's hands must not be tied when the Nation's life is in danger.

FRANKLIN DELANO ROOSEVELT, 32ND PRESIDENT (1933–1945)

Let every nation know, whether it wishes us well or ill, that we shall pay any price, bear any burden, meet any hardship, support any friend, oppose any foe to assure the survival and the success of liberty.

JOHN F. KENNEDY, 35TH PRESIDENT (1961–1963)

....

If we have to use force, it is because we are America. We are the indispensable nation. We stand tall. We see further into the future.

MADELEINE ALBRIGHT, FORMER SECRETARY OF STATE

We are called to defend liberty against tyranny and terror. We've answered that call. We will bring security to our people and justice to our enemies.

GEORGE W. BUSH, 43RD PRESIDENT (2001–)

The greatest danger of all would be to do nothing.

JOHN F. KENNEDY, 35TH PRESIDENT (1961–1963)

....

Our country's security doesn't depend on the heroism of every citizen. But we have to be worthy of the sacrifices made on our behalf.

JOHN McCAIN, U.S. SENATOR

....

Those who would give up essential Liberty, to purchase a little temporary Safety, deserve neither Liberty nor Safety.

BENJAMIN FRANKLIN, STATESMAN AND SCIENTIST

Our forbearance should never be misunderstood. Our reluctance for conflict should not be misjudged as a failure of will. When action is required to preserve our national security, we will act.

RONALD REAGAN, 40TH PRESIDENT (1981–1989)

Preparing for a far-off storm that may reach our shores is far wiser than ignoring the thunder until the clouds are just overhead.

WILLIAM J. CLINTON, 42ND PRESIDENT (1993–2001)

Hostilities exist. There is no blinking at the fact that our people, our territory, and our interests are in grave danger.

FRANKLIN DELANO ROOSEVELT, 32ND PRESIDENT (1933–1945)

It is through constant questioning we will stay the course, and that is a course that will ultimately defend our troops and protect our national security.

JOHN KERRY, U.S. SENATOR

SERVICE

You have to be willing to work very hard. It is not a soft life, it's a difficult life. It's a life of sacrifice, it's a life of service. That's why we call it service.

COLIN POWELL, FORMER SECRETARY OF STATE

Service to others is the rent you pay for your room here on earth.

MUHAMMAD ALI, FORMER WORLD HEAVYWEIGHT CHAMPION

I can truly and from my heart say that the most mortifying circumstance attendant upon my retirement from public life is that my power of doing good to my fellow creatures is curtailed and diminished, but though the means is wanting, the will and wish remain.

ABIGAIL ADAMS, FORMER FIRST LADY

Through the gathering momentum of millions of acts of kindness and decency, we will change America one soul at a time—and we will build a culture of service.

GEORGE W. BUSH, 43RD PRESIDENT (2001–)

Our country is built on what we, as individuals, bring to the public arena.

ELIZABETH DOLE, U.S. SENATOR AND 2000 REPUBLICAN PRESIDENTIAL CANDIDATE

The patriot volunteer, fighting for country and his rights, makes the most reliable soldier on earth.

STONEWALL JACKSON, U.S. AND CONFEDERATE ARMY OFFICER

A man who has never lost himself in a cause bigger than himself has missed one of life's mountaintop experiences. Only in losing himself does he find himself. Only then does he discover all the latent strengths he never knew he had and which would otherwise have remained dormant.

RICHARD M. NIXON, 37TH PRESIDENT (1969–1974)

....

And so, my fellow Americans: Ask not what your country can do for you—ask what you can do for your country.

JOHN F. KENNEDY, 35TH PRESIDENT (1961–1963)

....

I must admit that I personally measure success in terms of the contributions an individual makes to her or his fellow human beings.

MARGARET MEAD, ANTHROPOLOGIST

Time and money spent in helping men to do more for themselves is far better than mere giving.

HENRY FORD, INDUSTRIALIST AND AUTOMOBILE MANUFACTURER

It is not enough to understand, or to see clearly. The future will be shaped in the arena of human activity, by those willing to commit their minds and their bodies to the task.

ROBERT F. KENNEDY, FORMER ATTORNEY GENERAL AND U.S. SENATOR

I was constantly told and challenged to live my life as a warrior. As a warrior, you assume responsibility for yourself. The warrior humbles himself. And the warrior learns the power of giving.

BILLY MILLS, OLYMPIC GOLD MEDALIST

None of us get to where we are without standing on the shoulders of another. And none of us will get to where we need to go without bending down to lift up someone who comes after us.

DONNA E. SHALALA, FORMER SECRETARY OF HEALTH AND HUMAN SERVICES

....

One individual can make a world of difference ... even, I might say, a different world.

ELIZABETH DOLE, U.S. SENATOR

....

If we do not lay out ourselves in the service of mankind, whom should we serve?

JOHN ADAMS, 1ST VICE PRESIDENT (1789–1797) AND 2ND PRESIDENT (1797–1801)

America needs men and women who respond to the call of duty, who stand up for the weak, who speak up for their beliefs, who sacrifice for a great good.

GEORGE W. BUSH, 43RD PRESIDENT (2001–   )

....

Speak little, do much.

BENJAMIN FRANKLIN, STATESMAN AND SCIENTIST

....

I truly believe that I understand what faces the great masses of people in the country today. I have no illusions that anyone can change the world in a short time. ... Yet I do believe that even a few people, who want to understand, to help and to do the right thing for the great numbers of people instead of for the few can help.

ELEANOR ROOSEVELT, FORMER FIRST LADY AND UNITED NATIONS DELEGATE

Our success as a Nation depends upon our willingness to give generously of ourselves for the welfare and enrichment of the lives of others.

PAT NIXON, FORMER FIRST LADY

In this our country has, in my judgment, thus far fulfilled its highest duty to suffering humanity. It has spoken and will continue to speak, not only by its words, but by its acts, the language of sympathy, encouragement, and hope to those who earnestly listen to tones which pronounce for the largest rational liberty.

FRANKLIN PIERCE, 14TH PRESIDENT (1853–1857)

I believe in the goodness of a free society. And I believe that society can remain good only as long as we are willing to fight for it—and to fight against whatever imperfections may exist.

JACKIE ROBINSON, PROFESSIONAL BASEBALL PLAYER

The brave man inattentive to his duty is worth little more to his country than the coward who deserts her in the hour of danger.

ANDREW JACKSON, 7TH PRESIDENT (1829–1837)

When you cease to make a contribution, you begin to die.

ELEANOR ROOSEVELT, FORMER FIRST LADY

TERRORISM

*

Terror, unanswered, cannot only bring down buildings, it can threaten the stability of legitimate governments.

GEORGE W. BUSH, 43RD PRESIDENT (2001–   )

America stands at a crease in history—225-plus years behind us—we ask ourselves, what will the next 225 years bring? We're reminded every day by the loss of brave men and women who serve in the global war on terrorism that freedom isn't free.

GENERAL TOMMY FRANKS

Let us teach our children that the God of comfort is also the God of righteousness. Those who trouble their own house will inherit the wind. Justice will prevail.

WILLIAM J. CLINTON, 42ND PRESIDENT (1993–2001)

The best long-term deterrent to terrorism is the spread of our principles of freedom, democracy, the rule of law, and respect for human life. The more that spreads around the globe, the safer we will all be. These are very powerful ideas and once they gain a foothold, they cannot be stopped.

RUDOLPH GIULIANI, FORMER MAYOR OF NEW YORK CITY

The War on Terror is not a clash of civilizations. It is a clash of civilization against chaos; of the best hopes of humanity against dogmatic fears of progress and the future.

JOHN KERRY, U.S. SENATOR

No terrorist campaign standing on its own has ever won.

WILLIAM J. CLINTON, 42ND PRESIDENT (1993–2001)

There have been many dramatic changes in life, and this is a new one. [The war on terror] will challenge our commitment to an open society and democratic values—always difficult to reconcile in the best of circumstances, now more difficult, but I think possible.

GEORGE MITCHELL, FORMER U.S. SENATOR MAJORITY LEADER

Terrorism preys particularly on cultures and communities that practice openness and tolerance. Their targeting of innocent civilians mocks the efforts of those who seek to live together in peace as neighbors.

RUDOLPH GIULIANI, FORMER MAYOR OF NEW YORK CITY

A world free from terrorism's scourge, a world in which peace-loving nations no longer face blackmail or attack by rogue regimes, a Europe whole and free ... these are the objectives of our age. We are worthy of them.

JOHN MCCAIN, U.S. SENATOR

The war on terror must be fought on the offense.

CONDOLEEZZA RICE, SECRETARY OF STATE AND FORMER NATIONAL SECURITY ADVISOR

The only way to defeat terrorism as a threat to our way of life is to stop it, eliminate it, and destroy it where it grows.

GEORGE W. BUSH, 43RD PRESIDENT (2001–)

The global war on terrorism will be a long fight. But make no mistake about it: We are going to fight the terrorists.

GENERAL TOMMY FRANKS

Wherever terrorists operate, we must find them where they dwell, stop them in their planning, and one by one bring them to justice.

DICK CHENEY, 46TH VICE PRESIDENT (2001–)

....

The war on terrorism must be waged at every level, with every tool of state-craft, for as long as it takes.

COLIN POWELL, FORMER SECRETARY OF STATE

....

The battles against tyranny, terrorism, and weapons of mass destruction, and for freedom, opportunity, and security, are the great causes of our time, and the greatest alliance of all time must lead the way in winning those battles.

JOSEPH LIEBERMAN, U.S. SENATOR

We must come to terms with a fundamental truth—we have reached a point in history when the margin of error we once enjoyed is gone.

DONALD RUMSFELD, U.S. SECRETARY OF DEFENSE

Winning the War on Terror will not happen by military strength alone. This is fundamentally about America's values and leadership.

HILLARY RODHAM CLINTON, U.S. SENATOR AND FORMER FIRST LADY

We must rise to the challenge. We must rise to the challenge with actions that will rid the globe of terrorism and create a world in which all God's children can live without fear.

COLIN POWELL, FORMER SECRETARY OF STATE

As long as the United States of America is determined and strong, this will not be an age of terror; this will be an age of liberty, here and across the world.

GEORGE W. BUSH, 43RD PRESIDENT (2001–   )

We are now in a struggle with the soul of the 21st century.

WILLIAM J. CLINTON, 42ND PRESIDENT (1993–2001)

UNITY

—★—

Let us, then, fellow citizens, unite with one heart and one mind. Let us restore to social intercourse that harmony and affection without which liberty and even life itself are but dreary things.

THOMAS JEFFERSON, 3RD PRESIDENT (1801–1809)

We must all hang together or assuredly we shall all hang separately.

BENJAMIN FRANKLIN, STATESMAN AND SCIENTIST

The ultimate strength of our country and our cause will lie not in powerful weapons or infinite resources or boundless wealth, but will lie in the unity of our people.

LYNDON B. JOHNSON, 36TH PRESIDENT (1963–1969)

With God's help and for the sake of our Nation, it is time for us to join hands in America. Let us commit ourselves together to a rebirth of the American spirit. Working together with our common faith, we cannot fail.

JIMMY CARTER, 39TH PRESIDENT (1977–1981)

We face the arduous days that lie before us in the warm courage of national unity.

FRANKLIN DELANO ROOSEVELT, 32ND PRESIDENT (1933–1945)

I think it is very difficult for us to collectively and symbolically join hands and begin to move forward in solving this country's problems if we continue to have these stereotypes about one another.

WILMA MANKILLER, FORMER CHIEF OF THE CHEROKEE NATION

America has never been united by blood or birth or soil. We are bound by ideals that move us beyond our backgrounds, lift us above our interests and teach us what it means to be citizens. Every child must be taught these principles. Every citizen must uphold them. And every immigrant, by embracing these ideals, makes our country more, not less, American.

GEORGE W. BUSH, 43RD PRESIDENT (2001–)

Together we can widen the circle of opportunity for all Americans, transcend our differences and divisions, and give our children a safer and more secure future. That's the promise of America.

HILLARY RODHAM CLINTON, U.S. SENATOR AND FORMER FIRST LADY

....

There's not a liberal America and a conservative America—there's the United States of America.

OBAMA BARACK, U.S. SENATOR

Discipline isn't what causes men to go into the face of enemy fire, it's counting on one another, and serving one another, and loving one another as family members.

COLIN POWELL, FORMER SECRETARY OF STATE

....

We all do better when we work together. Our differences do matter but our common humanity matters more.

WILLIAM J. CLINTON, 42ND PRESIDENT (1993–2001)

....

Coming together is a beginning, keeping together is progress, working together is success.

HENRY FORD, INDUSTRIALIST AND AUTOMOBILE MANUFACTURER

Our American unity does not depend upon unanimity. We have differences; but now, as in the past, we can derive from those differences strength, not weakness, wisdom, not despair.

LYNDON B. JOHNSON, 36TH PRESIDENT (1963–1969)

We cannot be separated in interest or divided in purpose. We stand together until the end.

WOODROW WILSON, 28TH PRESIDENT (1913–1921)

Our American values are not luxuries but necessities, not the salt in our bread, but the bread itself. Our common vision of a free and just society is our greatest source of cohesion at home and strength abroad, greater than the bounty of our material blessings.

JIMMY CARTER, 39TH PRESIDENT (1977–1981)

....

Our strength is our unity of purpose.

FRANKLIN DELANO ROOSEVELT, 32ND PRESIDENT (1933–1945)

....

The American people have encountered together great dangers and sustained severe trials with success. They constitute one great family with a common interest.

JAMES MONROE, 5TH PRESIDENT (1817–1825)

What we need in the United States is not division; what we need in the United States is not hatred; what we need in the United States is not violence and lawlessness; but with love and wisdom, and compassion toward one another, and a feeling of justice toward those who still suffer within our country, whether they be white or whether they be black.

ROBERT F. KENNEDY, FORMER ATTORNEY GENERAL AND U.S. SENATOR

There is no way we can go forward except together and no way anybody can win except by serving the people's urgent needs.

GERALD R. FORD, 38TH PRESIDENT (1974–1977)

The time has come for Americans of all races and creeds and political beliefs to understand and to respect one another.

LYNDON B. JOHNSON, 36TH PRESIDENT (1963–1969)

You will find men who want to be carried on the shoulders of others, who think that the world owes them a living. They don't seem to see that we must all lift together and pull together.

HENRY FORD, INDUSTRIALIST AND AUTOMOBILE MANUFACTURER

At the heart of all that civilization has meant and developed is "community"— the mutually cooperative and voluntary venture of man to assume a semblance of responsibility for his brother.

MARTIN LUTHER KING, JR., CIVIL RIGHTS LEADER

....

America is nothing if it consists of each of us. It is something only if it consists of all of us.

WOODROW WILSON, 28TH PRESIDENT (1913–1921)

....

Individual commitment to a group effort—that is what makes a team work, a company work, a society work, a civilization work.

VINCE LOMBARDI, FORMER FOOTBALL COACH

I think America discovered something about itself [on September 11th], about how much we could help each other, how much we care about each other, how much we care about being Americans, how important our freedom and democracy is to us.

RUDOLPH GIULIANI, FORMER MAYOR OF NEW YORK CITY

We must go forward as one nation.

WILLIAM J. CLINTON, 42ND PRESIDENT (1993–2001)

All mankind is tied together; all life is interrelated, and we are all caught in an inescapable network of mutuality, tied in a single garment of destiny.

MARTIN LUTHER KING, JR., CIVIL RIGHTS LEADER

America is in need of unity and longing for a larger measure of compassion.

JOHN KERRY, U.S. SENATOR

....

Global unity through global diversity is also the future of mankind.

BILLY MILLS, OLYMPIC GOLD MEDALIST

....

A person in crisis often needs more than a program or a check; he needs a friend.

GEORGE W. BUSH, 43RD PRESIDENT (2001–)

With all of our differences, whenever we are confronted with a threat to our security we are not then Republicans or Democrats but Americans; we are not then fifty states but the United States.

RICHARD M. NIXON, 37TH PRESIDENT (1969–1974)

....

If we are to live together in peace, we must come to know each other better.

LYNDON B. JOHNSON, 36TH PRESIDENT (1963–1969)

....

We believe we must be the family of America, recognizing that at the heart of the matter we are bound one to another.

MARIO CUOMO, FORMER GOVERNOR OF NEW YORK

We are a nation of many nationalities, many races, many religions—bound together by a single unity, the unity of freedom and equality. Whoever seeks to set one nationality against another, seeks to degrade all nationalities.

FRANKLIN DELANO ROOSEVELT, 32ND PRESIDENT (1933–1945)

You cannot become thorough Americans if you think of yourselves in groups. America does not consist of groups. A man who thinks of himself as belonging to a particular national group in America has not yet become an American.

WOODROW WILSON, 28TH PRESIDENT (1913–1921)

People who work together will win, whether it be against complex football defenses, or the problems of modern society.

VINCE LOMBARDI, FORMER FOOTBALL COACH

We can continue building our bridge to tomorrow. It will require some red American line drawing and some blue American barrier breaking, but we can do it together.

WILLIAM J. CLINTON, 42ND PRESIDENT (1993–2001)

We must learn to live together as brothers or perish together as fools.

MARTIN LUTHER KING, JR., CIVIL RIGHTS LEADER

....

In our strength we rose together, rallied our energies together, applied the old rules of common sense, and together survived.

FRANKLIN DELANO ROOSEVELT, 32ND PRESIDENT (1933–1945)

....

We must build one America. We must be one America, strong and united for another very important reason—because we are at war.

JOHN EDWARDS, FORMER U.S. SENATOR

Our nation relies on men and women who look after a neighbor and surround the lost with love.

GEORGE W. BUSH, 43RD PRESIDENT (2001–   )

One of America's finest traditions is our ability to draw together in support of our men and women in uniform when they are actively engaged in the defense of our freedom.

JOHN MCCAIN, U.S. SENATOR

Our unity need not be a uniformity of tactics or views, but rather a union of purpose. Those who cherish free political systems and free economic systems share similar hopes. And working together, those hopes can be realities for the many more who yearn to be free.

DONALD RUMSFELD, U.S. SECRETARY OF DEFENSE

WAR

—★—

The consequences of war are dire, the sacrifices immeasurable. We may have occasion in our lifetime to once again rise up in defense of our freedom, and pay the wages of war. But we ought not—we will not—travel down that hellish path blindly.

OBAMA BARACK, U.S. SENATOR

Wars are to be avoided, but when they have to be fought, fight them well and get them over with quickly. With all the exhilaration and joy that comes from victory and success, don't ever forget the price that was paid for it.

COLIN POWELL, FORMER SECRETARY OF STATE

It is a fearful thing to lead this great peaceful people into war, into the most terrible and disastrous to all wards, civilization itself seeming to be in the balance.

WOODROW WILSON, 28TH PRESIDENT (1913–1921)

Let's get out of the fevered delirium of war, with the hallucination that all the money in the world is to be made in the madness of war and the wildness of its aftermath.

WARREN G. HARDING, 29TH PRESIDENT (1921–1923)

Total war makes no sense in an age when great powers can maintain large and relatively invulnerable nuclear forces and refuse to surrender without resort to those forces.

JOHN F. KENNEDY, 35TH PRESIDENT (1961–1963)

Older men declare war. But it is youth that must fight and die. And it is youth who must inherit the tribulation, the sorrow, and the triumphs that are the aftermath of war.

HERBERT HOOVER, 31ST PRESIDENT (1929–1933)

War is an invention of the human mind. The human mind can invent peace with justice.

NORMAN COUSINS, EDITOR AND WRITER

....

I hate war as only a soldier who has lived it can, only as one who has seen its brutality, its futility, its stupidity.

DWIGHT D. EISENHOWER, 34TH PRESIDENT (1953–1961)

....

However horrible the incidents of war may be, the soldier who is called upon to offer and to give his life for his country is the noblest development of mankind.

GENERAL DOUGLAS MACARTHUR

Americans love to fight, traditionally. All real Americans love the sting and clash of battle. America loves a winner. America will not tolerate a loser. Americans despise a coward; Americans play to win. That's why America has never lost and never will lose a war.

GENERAL GEORGE S. PATTON

....

Either war is obsolete or men are.

R. BUCKMINSTER FULLER, ARCHITECT AND ENGINEER

....

War is an awful business. The lives of a nation's finest patriots are sacrificed. Innocent people suffer. Commerce is disrupted. Economies are damaged. Strategic interests shielded by years of statecraft are endangered as the demands of war and diplomacy conflict. However just the cause, we should shed a tear for all that is lost when war claims its wages from us.

JOHN MCCAIN, U.S. SENATOR

Whenever we depart from voluntary cooperation and try to do good by using force, the bad moral value of force triumphs over good intentions.

MILTON FRIEDMAN, NOBEL PRIZE-WINNING ECONOMIST

We fight because we must fight if we are to live in a world where every country can shape its own destiny. And only in such a world will our own freedom be finally secure.

LYNDON B. JOHNSON, 36TH PRESIDENT (1963–1969)

If the outcome of war depended upon ideals alone, this would be a different world than it is today.

CHARLES LINDBERGH, AVIATOR AND PULITZER PRIZE-WINNING AUTHOR

In every battle there comes a time when both sides consider themselves beaten, then he who continues the attack wins.

ULYSSES S. GRANT, 18TH PRESIDENT (1869–1877)

Neutrality is no longer feasible or desirable where the peace of the world is involved and the freedom of its peoples. ...

WOODROW WILSON, 28TH PRESIDENT (1913–1921)

Even the lesson of victory itself brings with it profound concern, both for our future security and the survival of civilization. The destructiveness of the war potential, through progressive advances in scientific discovery, has in fact now reached a point which revises the traditional concepts of war.

GENERAL DOUGLAS MACARTHUR

....

All of us who served in one war or another know very well that all wars are the glory and the agony of the young.

GERALD R. FORD, 38TH PRESIDENT (1974–1977)

We can't make victory on the battlefield harder to achieve so that our diplomacy is easier to conduct.

JOHN MCCAIN, U.S. SENATOR

....

Anyone who tells you that one political party has a monopoly on the defense of our nation is committing a fraud on the American people.

GENERAL WESLEY K. CLARK

....

I love peace, and I am anxious that we should give the world still another useful lesson, by showing to them other modes of punishing injuries than by war, which is as much a punishment to the punisher as to the sufferer.

THOMAS JEFFERSON, 3RD PRESIDENT (1801–1809)

It is essential to understand that battles are primarily won in the hearts of men.

VINCE LOMBARDI, FORMER FOOTBALL COACH

May we never see another war! For in my opinion, there never was a good war or a bad peace.

BENJAMIN FRANKLIN, STATESMAN AND SCIENTIST

An Army is a team, lives, sleeps, fights, and eats as a team. This individual hero stuff is a lot of horse shit! ... Every single man in the Army plays a vital role. Every man has his job to do and must do it.

GENERAL GEORGE S. PATTON

People don't start wars, governments do.

RONALD REAGAN, 40TH PRESIDENT (1981–1989)

War may sometimes be a necessary evil. But no matter how necessary, it is always an evil, never a good. We will not learn how to live together in peace by killing each other's children.

JIMMY CARTER, 39TH PRESIDENT (1977–1981)

In time of war, truth is always replaced by propaganda.

CHARLES LINDBERGH, AVIATOR AND PULITZER PRIZE-WINNING AUTHOR

....

Mankind must put an end to war, or war will put an end to mankind.

JOHN F. KENNEDY, 35TH PRESIDENT (1961–1963)

....

We are now engaged in a great Civil War, testing whether this nation or any nation so conceived and so dedicated can long endure.

ABRAHAM LINCOLN, 16TH PRESIDENT (1861–1865)

There is one choice we cannot make, we are incapable of making—we will not choose the path of submission and suffer the most sacred rights of our nation and our people to be ignored or violated.

Woodrow Wilson, 28th President (1913–1921)

I have never advocated war except as a means of peace.

Ulysses S. Grant, 18th President (1869–1877)

....

It is fatal to enter any war without the will to win it.

General Douglas MacArthur

....

We will not prematurely or unnecessarily risk the costs of worldwide nuclear war in which even the fruits of victory would be ashes in our mouth.

John F. Kennedy, 35th President (1961–1963)

When all is said and done, and statesmen discuss the future of the world, the fact remains that people fight these wars.

Eleanor Roosevelt, Former First Lady and United Nations Delegate

Almost any man worthy of his salt would fight to defend his home, but no one ever heard of a man going to war for his boarding house.

Mark Twain, Author and Humorist

That no man should scruple, or hesitate a moment to use arms in defense of so valuable a blessing [as freedom], on which all the good and evil of life depends, is clearly my opinion; yet arms ... should be the last resort.

GEORGE WASHINGTON, 1ST PRESIDENT (1789–1797)

Wars can be prevented just as surely as they can be provoked, and we who fail to prevent them must share in the guilt for the dead.

GENERAL OMAR N. BRADLEY

The United States of America never goes to war because we want to, we only go to war because we have to.

JOHN KERRY, U.S. SENATOR

There can be no tougher decision—no tougher decision—than the decision to go to war, the decision to put our sons and daughters into harm's way.

GENERAL TOMMY FRANKS

In this age there can be no losers in peace and no victors in war, we must recognize the obligation to match national strength with national restraint.

LYNDON B. JOHNSON, 36TH PRESIDENT (1963–1969)

....

More than an end to war, we want an end to the beginning of all wars.

FRANKLIN DELANO ROOSEVELT, 32ND PRESIDENT (1933–1945)

Wars may be fought with weapons but they are won by men. It is the spirit of the men who follow and of the man who leads that gains the victory.

GENERAL GEORGE S. PATTON

To such a task we can dedicate our lives and our fortunes, everything that we are and everything that we have, with the pride of those who know that the day has come when America is privileged to spend her blood and her might for the principles that gave her birth and happiness and the peace which she has treasured.

WOODROW WILSON, 28TH PRESIDENT (1913–1921)

If America cannot win a war in a week, it begins negotiating with itself.

THOMAS PAINE, AMERICAN REVOLUTIONARY LEADER

....

When you fight a war, there is one rule you always follow: You never, ever leave a soldier behind.

GENERAL WESLEY K. CLARK

....

And in the end, through the long ages of our quest for light, it will be found that truth is still mightier than the sword.

GENERAL DOUGLAS MACARTHUR

Never think that war, no matter how necessary, nor how justified, is not a crime.

ERNEST HEMINGWAY, NOBEL PRIZE-WINNING AUTHOR

....

War is cruelty, and you cannot refine it.

WILLIAM TECUMSEH SHERMAN, AMERICAN CIVIL WAR GENERAL

....

So long as there are men there will be wars.

ALBERT EINSTEIN, NOBEL PRIZE-WINNING PHYSICIST

No matter how long it may take us to overcome this premeditated invasion, the American people in their righteous might will win through to absolute victory.

FRANKLIN DELANO ROOSEVELT, 32ND PRESIDENT (1933–1945)

War is fear cloaked in courage.

GENERAL WILLIAM C. WESTMORELAND

Great is the guilt of an unnecessary war.

JOHN ADAMS, 1ST VICE PRESIDENT (1789–1797) AND 2ND PRESIDENT (1797–1801)

YOUTH

— ⭐ —

Fortunately for us and our world, youth is not easily discouraged. Youth with its clear vista and boundless faith and optimism is uninhibited by the thousands of considerations that always bedevil man in his progress. The hopes of the world rest on the flexibility, vigor, capacity for new thought, the fresh outlook of the young.

DWIGHT D. EISENHOWER, 34TH PRESIDENT (1953–1961)

If you can bring to your children the self that you truly are, as opposed to some amalgam of manners and mannerisms, expectations and fears that you have acquired as a carapace along the way, you will give them, too, a great gift.

ANNA QUINDLEN, AUTHOR

The advice I would give any young person is, first of all, to rid themselves of prejudice against other people and to be concerned about what they can do to help others.

ROSA PARKS, CIVIL RIGHTS PIONEER

You today are smarter than we were. You are better educated and better informed than we were twenty-five years ago. And that is part of your heritage.

RONALD REAGAN, 40TH PRESIDENT (1981–1989)

We are grateful that we can trust in the youth of the nation that they are going on to uphold the real principles of democracy and put them into action in this country. They are going to make us an even more truly democratic nation.

ELEANOR ROOSEVELT, FORMER FIRST LADY AND UNITED NATIONS DELEGATE

It is the prerogative of youth to believe that things will go well, that all one has to do is the right thing and everything will turn out fine.

ALAN KEYES, FORMER U.S. REPRESENTATIVE TO THE UNITED NATIONS

This world demands the qualities of youth: not a time of life but a state of mind, a temper of the will, a quality of imagination, a predominance of courage over timidity, of the appetite for adventure over the love of ease.

ROBERT F. KENNEDY, FORMER ATTORNEY GENERAL AND U.S. SENATOR

....

On you depend the fortunes of America. You are to decide the important questions upon which rests the happiness and the liberty of millions yet unborn. Act worthy of yourselves.

DR. JOSEPH WARREN, AMERICAN REVOLUTIONARY LEADER

You will determine whether we become a culture of selfishness and look inward—or whether we will embrace a culture of service and look outward.

GEORGE W. BUSH, 43RD PRESIDENT (2001–)

The children of this country can learn in a profound way that integrity is important and selfishness is wrong.

WILLIAM J. CLINTON, 42ND PRESIDENT (1993–2001)

....

We have a responsibility to base every decision we make about our future on the answer to one simple question: Will it be good for our children?

GENERAL WESLEY K. CLARK

....

We are obligated to leave as good a future as we can for our children. The other side of that coin is that they will inherit the future and be responsible for running things. We need to make sure they're qualified.

LEE BROWN, FORMER DIRECTOR OF THE OFFICE OF DRUG CONTROL POLICY

INDEX

A

Adams, Abigail, 72, 214

Adams, Henry, 184

Adams, John, 37, 81, 96, 100, 107, 114, 123, 164, 166, 169, 188, 216, 241

Adams, John Quincy, 72, 81, 98, 155

Adams, Samuel, 99

Albright, Madeleine, 58, 82, 84, 134, 189, 190, 211

Ali, Muhammad, 11, 15, 17, 44, 54, 173, 194, 214

Angelou, Maya, 15, 56, 72, 129

Anthony, Susan B., 22, 82

Armstrong, Neil, 195

Arthur, Chester A., 206

Ashcroft, John, 37, 136, 153

Asimov, Isaac, 67

B

Baldwin, James, 45

Ballard, Robert, 15, 21, 142, 144, 155

Bancroft, George, 64

Barack, Obama, 8, 126, 154, 224, 232

Beecher, Henry Ward, 20, 37

Bradley, Omar N., 239

Brandeis, Louis, 14, 34, 95, 98, 116, 195

Brooks, Phillips, 19

Brown, Lee, 244

Bryan, William Jennings, 32, 109, 163, 167

Buchanan, James, 81

Buck, Pearl S., 113, 127

Bush, Barbara, 16, 23, 35

Bush, George H.W., 1, 3, 7, 107, 118, 173, 191, 193

Bush, George W., 29, 33, 87, 88, 90, 98, 101, 105, 114, 127, 132, 148, 150, 152, 164, 166, 169, 170, 209, 210, 212, 214, 217, 219, 221, 222, 224, 228, 231, 244

Bush, Laura, 108

C

Calhoun, John C., 96

Carnegie, Andrew, 25, 28, 135

Carnegie, Dale, 126

Carson, Johnny, 193

Carter, Jimmy, 8, 10, 30, 59, 61, 63, 107, 109, 113, 115, 119, 123, 130, 134, 146, 148, 156, 165, 184, 199, 209, 223, 226, 237

Carter, Rosalyn, 11

Catt, Carrie Chapman, 151

Channing, William Ellery, 54

Cheney, Dick, 2, 102, 108, 128, 155, 221

Chomsky, Noam, 68, 142

Clark, Wesley K., 236, 240, 244

Clay, Henry, 51

Cleveland, Grover, 30, 62

Clinton, Hillary Rodham, 11, 65, 82, 84, 95, 222, 224

Clinton, William J., 1, 7, 109, 145, 160, 173, 183, 191, 205, 207, 213, 219, 220, 222, 225, 228, 230, 244

Coolidge, Calvin, 4, 29, 51, 86, 89, 90, 100, 112, 122, 135, 144, 162

Cooper, James Fennimore, 37, 79

Cousins, Norman, 233

Crockett, Davy, 120

Cuomo, Mario, 161, 183, 229

Curtis, George William, 168

D

Darrow, Clarence, 193

Dean, Howard, 198

Debs, Eugene, 69

Delay, Tom, 119, 135

Denton, Jeremiah A., 20, 60, 118

Dewey, John, 143

Dewey, Thomas, 186

Disney, Walt, 134

Dole, Bob, 102, 158

Dole, Elizabeth, 214, 216

Dos Passos, John, 106

Douglass, Frederick, 45, 73, 196, 201

Dove, Rita, 143, 144, 197

DuBois, W.E.B., 43, 49, 50

Dulles, John Foster, 174, 176

E

Earhart, Amelia, 55

Eastwood, Clint, 189

Edison, Thomas, 132, 136, 172, 181, 196

Edwards, John, 166, 230

Einstein, Albert, 39, 97, 113, 138, 142, 197, 241

Eisenhower, Dwight D., 1, 5, 22, 31, 51, 59, 68, 101, 103, 107, 116, 137, 146, 149, 164, 173, 174, 176, 178, 180, 182, 184, 193, 204, 209, 210, 233, 242

Eliot, Charles W., 72

Emerson, Ralph Waldo, 19, 55, 73, 76, 86, 92, 176, 188, 196

F

Faulkner, William, 95, 101, 127

Ferraro, Geraldine, 83, 110, 175

Flynt, Larry, 116

Ford, Gerald R., 10, 52, 111, 120, 162, 169, 192, 202, 226, 235

Ford, Henry, 21, 23, 26, 28, 75, 134, 196, 198, 200, 215, 225, 227

Franken, Al, 38

Franklin, Benjamin, 52, 73, 74, 77, 91, 149, 167, 168, 177, 211, 212, 217, 223, 236

Franks, Tommy, 160, 219, 221, 239

Friedman, Milton, 62, 234

Fulghum, Robert, 181

Fuller, R. Buckminster, 88, 136, 139, 159, 197, 200, 234

G

Gaines, Ernest J., 67

Galbraith, John Kenneth, 187

Gardner, John, 125

Garfield, James, 25, 74, 111, 115, 134

Garrison, William Lloyd, 45

Gherig, Lou, 43

Gingrich, Newt, 24
Giuliani, Rudolph,
    3, 91, 104, 128,
    137, 154, 219,
    220, 228
Glenn, John, 59,
    74
Goldin, Daniel S.,
    156, 198
Goldwater, Barry,
    102, 158
Goodwin, Doris
    Kearns, 186
Gore, Al, 3, 11, 22,
    33, 58, 60, 63,
    122, 127, 134,
    137, 186, 190,
    192
Graham, Billy, 14,
    24, 55
Grant, Ulysses S.,
    58, 182, 197,
    235, 238
Greeley, Horace, 19
Greenspan, Alan, 19
Grimké, Angelina,
    46

H

Hale, Nathan, 162
Hamilton,
    Alexander, 52,
    120, 125, 150

Hancock, John, 66
Hand, Learned, 97
Harding, Warren
    G., 5, 92, 109,
    114, 117, 232
Harlan, John
    Marshall, 42
Harrison,
    Benjamin, 125,
    202
Harrison, Caroline,
    82
Harrison, William
    Henry, 124
Hayes, Rutherford
    B., 122
Hayes, Woody, 3
Hazlitt, Henry, 99
Helms, Jesse, 189
Hemingway, Ernest,
    241
Henry, Patrick, 52,
    93, 101, 103
Heston, Charlton,
    67
Holmes, Oliver
    Wendell, 58
Holmes, Oliver
    Wendell, Jr., 20
Hoover, Herbert,
    31, 40, 116, 129,
    163, 177, 178,
    186, 233

Hoover, Lou
    Henry, 32
Hope, Bob, 73, 75
Humphrey, Hubert,
    9, 42, 60, 69,
    83, 121, 159, 182,
    185

I

Iacocca, Lee, 23, 74
Ickes, Herald, 2, 9,
    101, 110

J

Jackson, Andrew,
    17, 32, 53, 117,
    119, 160, 177,
    201, 218
Jackson, Jesse, 42,
    140, 155, 205
Jackson, Robert H.,
    117
Jackson, Stonewall,
    215
Jay, John, 103
Jefferson, Thomas,
    4, 18, 25, 28,
    38, 40, 51, 64,
    67, 75, 76, 78,
    90, 93, 96, 103,
    106, 110, 115,
    121, 123, 124,
    131, 138, 140,

150, 162, 189,
    195, 223, 236
Jennings, Peter, 184
Johnson, Lady Bird,
    56
Johnson, Lyndon
    B., 13, 14, 43,
    45, 46, 49, 54,
    79, 80, 92, 110,
    126, 129, 133,
    163, 167, 169,
    170, 177, 178,
    180, 191, 192,
    203, 205, 207,
    208, 210, 223,
    225, 227, 229,
    234, 239
Jordan, Michael,
    13, 14, 50

K

Keller, Helen, 18
Kennedy, Anthony
    M., 103, 198
Kennedy, Edward
    M., 2, 87, 89,
    105, 121, 122,
    124
Kennedy, John F.,
    8, 17, 20, 46,
    65, 69, 74, 76,
    79, 80, 91, 100,
    106, 112, 117,

124, 127, 128,
133, 143, 144,
146, 149, 152,
161, 163, 165,
172, 174, 176,
179, 180, 182,
194, 196, 200,
202, 205, 207,
209, 211, 212,
215, 233, 237,
238
Kennedy, Robert F.,
6, 13, 22, 31,
44, 46, 62, 66,
107, 113, 123,
130, 132, 181,
204, 216, 226,
243
Kerry, John, 16,
79, 86, 108,
142, 187, 210,
213, 220, 228,
239
Keyes, Alan, 57,
89, 93, 243
King, Jr., Martin
Luther, 13, 21,
33, 42, 44, 47,
70, 75, 78, 86,
88, 94, 103,
109, 129, 140,
147, 151, 152,
174, 178, 181,

199, 202, 206,
208, 227, 228,
230
Kissinger, Henry,
124, 131, 156,
158, 187
Krulak, Charles C.,
25, 54, 157
Kuhn, Maggie, 188

L
LaFollette, Robert,
38, 68
Landers, Ann, 19
Lee, Harper, 29,
53, 69
Lee, Robert E., 71
Lewis, Sinclair, 162
Lieberman, Joseph,
221
Limbaugh, Rush, 151
Lincoln, Abraham,
12, 18, 24, 26,
33, 45, 60, 75,
78, 80, 93, 98,
112, 121, 126,
139, 142, 160,
168, 171, 180,
189, 206, 237
Lincoln, Mary
Todd, 130
Lindbergh, Charles,
146, 235, 237

Lippmann, Walter,
138
Lowell, James
Russell, 199
Lombardi, Vince,
26, 29, 157,
227, 230, 236

M
MacArthur,
Douglas, 3, 5,
172, 175, 177,
179, 182, 205,
211, 233, 235,
238, 240
MacLeish,
Archibald, 91
Madison, Dolly
Todd, 185
Madison, James,
39, 75, 76, 116,
151, 190
Mankiller, Wilma,
224
Marshall, George
C., 26
Marshall,
Thurgood, 41,
120
Marx, Groucho,
184, 187
McCain, John, 13,
16, 53, 55, 70,

79, 96, 102,
105, 108, 133,
141, 161, 170,
183, 190, 206,
212, 220, 231,
234, 236
McGovern, George,
185
McKinley, William,
26, 119, 140
Mead, Margaret,
33, 76, 83, 85,
88, 215
Mills, Billy, 21, 216,
228
Mitchell, George,
173, 220
Monroe, James, 78,
111, 123, 226
Moran, Jerry, 112,
117, 137
Moore, Michael, 41
Moynihan, Daniel
Patrick, 118
Murrow, Edward
R., 68, 97, 125

N
Nader, Ralph, 17,
30, 32, 35, 153,
155, 197
Nelson, Gaylord, 64
Nixon, Pat, 12, 217

Nixon, Richard M.,
2, 7, 15, 27, 61,
65, 91, 139,
145, 165, 175,
176, 178, 180,
191, 203, 215,
229

O

O'Connor, Sandra
Day, 22, 34, 70
O'Douglas,
William, 72
Oppenheimer, J.
Robert, 39, 41,
73
O'Reilly, Bill, 120
O'Rourke, P.J., 70

Q

Quindlen, Anna,
242

P

Paine, Thomas, 34,
74, 92, 98, 111,
138, 141, 208,
240
Palmer, Arnold, 27
Parks, Rosa, 43, 47,
48, 53, 132, 242
Patton, George S.,
24, 69, 142,

157, 234, 237,
240
Paul, Alice, 84
Pelosi, Nancy, 3
Pepper, Claude, 62
Pierce, Franklin,
88, 175, 217
Polk, James, 192
Powell, Colin, 1, 12,
16, 26, 28, 31,
33, 66, 81, 127,
130, 145, 146,
149, 154, 156,
158, 184, 188,
208, 214, 221,
222, 225, 232
Presley, Elvis, 29

R

Rand, Ayn, 95
Rather, Dan, 10, 56
Reagan, Nancy, 141
Reagan, Ronald, 4,
7, 14, 17, 21, 23,
24, 38, 47, 55,
57, 61, 63, 94,
96, 101, 104,
108, 111, 112,
114, 119, 125,
128, 138, 154,
160, 163, 165,
166, 169, 171,
172, 180, 186,

192, 194, 206,
210, 212, 237,
242
Reeve, Christopher,
12, 19, 20
Reno, Janet, 62
Retton, Mary Lou,
24
Rice, Condoleezza,
2, 6, 45, 61,
64, 90, 93,
94, 100, 132,
136, 147, 194,
220
Ridge, Tom, 157
Robinson, Jackie,
27, 48, 218
Rockefeller, John
D., 29, 37, 39
Rockefeller, Nelson,
6
Rogers, Will, 187
Roosevelt, Eleanor,
28, 36, 38, 55,
58, 77, 83, 84,
86, 128, 133,
137, 141, 152,
179, 217, 218,
238, 243
Roosevelt, Franklin
Delano, 9, 27,
51, 52, 56, 59,
61, 71, 92, 95,

97, 99, 104, 115,
126, 129, 135,
136, 143, 147,
151, 156, 164,
170, 174, 191,
195, 197, 199,
203, 211, 213,
223, 226, 229,
230, 239, 241
Roosevelt,
Theodore, 6,
13, 18, 20, 23,
25, 31, 35, 36,
69, 71, 80, 95,
114, 117, 122,
131, 140, 151,
158, 163, 167,
183, 185, 187,
201
Rumsfeld, Donald,
121, 158, 196,
222, 231

S

Safire, William, 71
Santayana, George,
138
Sawyer, Diane, 81,
133
Schurz, Carl, 135,
164
Schwarzenegger,
Arnold, 167

Schwarzkopf, H. Norman, 53, 54, 155, 159
Scott, Hazel, 47
Shalala, Donna E., 32, 216
Sharpton, Al, 130
Shaw, Anna Howard, 83, 84
Shelton, Henry H., 15, 19, 195
Shepard, Jr., Alan, 143, 194, 207
Sherman, William Tecumseh, 57, 241
Simmons, Charles, 18
Smith, Margaret Chase, 67
Stanton, Elizabeth Cady, 30, 85
Steinbeck, John, 77, 131
Steinberg, Saul, 5
Steinem, Gloria, 188
Stevenson, Adlai, 10, 38, 40, 66, 68, 81, 87, 99, 110, 161, 168, 170, 178, 185, 200, 201

Stone, Lucy, 85, 140
Stowe, Harriet Beecher, 35

T

Taft, Helen, 85
Taft, William Howard, 40
Thomas, Clarence, 27, 49, 56, 167
Thoreau, Henry David, 66, 73, 139
Truman, Harry S., 60, 99, 118, 145, 147, 148, 152, 159, 192, 203
Tubman, Harriet, 43, 97
Twain, Mark, 78, 118, 162, 165, 198, 238

V

Van Buren, Martin, 35

W

Walker, Alice, 87, 203

Wallace, Mike, 9
Walton, Sam, 156
Warren, Joseph, 243
Washington, Booker T., 12, 16, 44, 46, 48, 50, 65
Washington, George, 39, 63, 64, 105, 115, 133, 145, 147, 148, 153, 168, 180, 187, 239
Washington, Martha, 17
Watts, J.C., 7, 70
Webster, Daniel, 41, 77, 94, 99, 106, 152, 161
Westmoreland, William C., 241
White, E.B., 8
White, William Allen, 105
Whitman, Walt, 2, 6, 10, 91, 153, 159
Wiesel, Elie, 90
Wilson, Woodrow, 1, 4, 8, 30, 57, 59, 63, 71, 93, 102, 104, 124, 140, 148, 150, 172,

175, 176, 179, 181, 204, 207, 208, 225, 227, 229, 232, 235, 238, 240
Winfrey, Oprah, 15, 21, 25, 76, 139, 190
Wolfowitz, Paul, 100
Wooden, John, 28, 34
Woodward, Bob, 9, 40
Wright, Frank Lloyd, 36, 96
X, Malcolm, 48, 50, 67, 77, 94, 100, 153, 190

Z

Zinn, Howard, 80, 120